Donna Robertson, Publisher
Fran Rohus, Design Director
Ange Workman, Production Director

Editorial
Jennifer A. Simcik, Senior Editor
Sharon Lothrop, Editor

Photography
Tammy Cromer-Campbell, Mary Craft
Photographers
Ruth Whitaker, Photo Stylist/Coordinator

Production/Book Design
Glenda Chamberlain, Production Manager

Production Team
Debby Keel, Betty Radla, Jean Schrecengost

Product Design
Brenda Wendling, Design Coordinator

Business
John Robinson, CEO
Karen Pierce, Vice President/Customer Service
Greg Deily, Vice President/Marketing
John Trotter, Vice President/M.I.S.

Credits
Sincerest thanks to all the designers,
manufacturers and other professionals whose
dedication has made this book possible.
Special thanks to Lori Powers of
R.R. Donnelley & Sons Co., Chicago, IL.

Library of Congress Cataloging-in-Publication Data
ISBN: 0-9638031-5-8
First Printing: 1995
Library of Congress Catalog Card Number: 94-69128
Published and Distributed by
The Needlecraft Shop, LLC.
Printed in the United States of America.

*D*ear Friends —

Inspiration is a fantastic feeling! And when I'm inspired about something new and exciting, I just can't wait to share it with all my friends. Within the pages of this book, I think you'll find a treasure trove of afghans so wonderful even those who don't crochet will be inspired by their beauty. From classic favorites to sleek contemporary styles, this collection is a must for your personal pattern library.

Leaf through these pages and you'll find yourself embarking on a crochet odyssey you've only dreamed of in the past. We've assembled these spectacular never-before-published creations from some of the industry's most artistic designers — just for you. Let yourself relish the same inspiration I experienced as you behold stunning, innovative afghans suitable for every occasion and every desire.

Whether you're a novice or a skilled artisan in your own right, you won't be able to resist the urge to possess every one of these superb examples of needlecraft's finest offerings. And the full-page color photographs and clear instructions, complete with detailed stitch information, will guide you on your adventure.

I hope you find this unique volume as inspirational as I did. Filled to the brim with an unforgettable sampling of the best crochet has to offer, its magical appeal is sure to captivate all who venture within its covers. Come along, and let it take you on the afghan excursion of your lifetime.

Happy Crocheting,

Jennifer

Country Garden

Lavish Lace

Patchwork Quilts

Sweet Dreams

Shades of Beauty

Contents

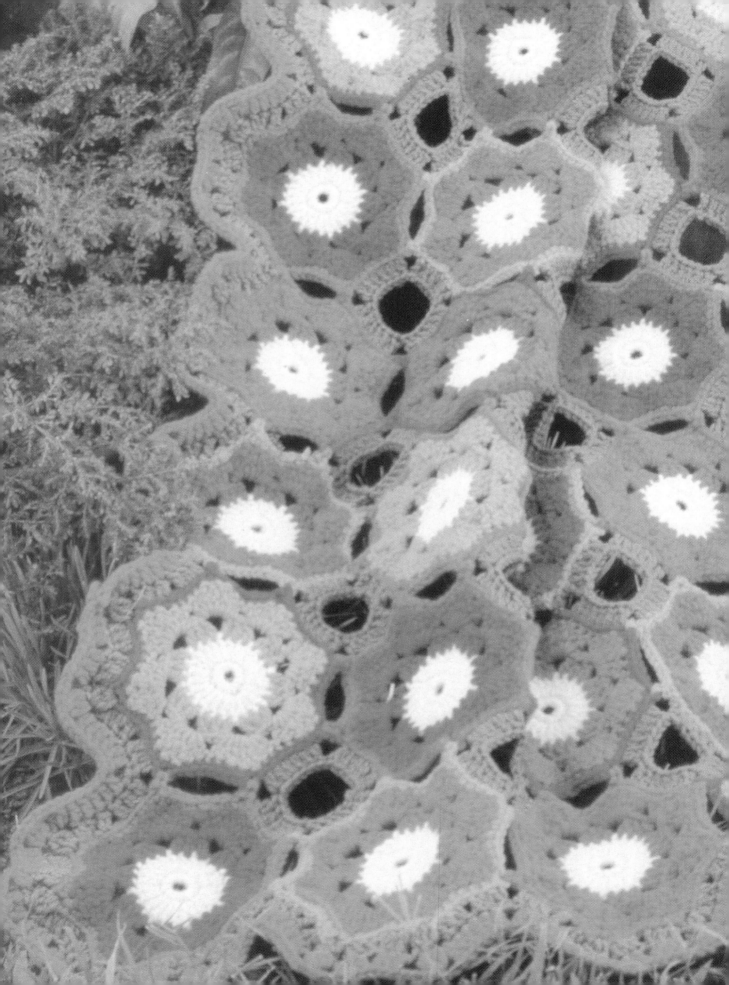

Country Garden

Journey into an enchantingly romantic garden bursting forth in an exquisite array of lush, colorful buds and blossoms. You'll thrill to the sensation of never-ending summer with these fresh-as-a-daisy designs guaranteed to keep your heart in bloom.

Cabbage Roses

jan hatfield, designer

Let your mind wander to thoughts of romance with this enchanting cover. The lacy nostalgic design has a mystical quality enhanced by rings of luscious roses.

Finished Size
51" x 68½"

Materials
Worsted-weight yarn — 48 oz. variegated, 25 oz. off-white and 9½ oz. dk. rose; tapestry needle; G and H crochet hooks or sizes needed to obtain gauges.

Gauge
G hook, 1 Rose on Ring is 4" across. H hook, 7 sts = 2"; 2 dc rows = 1".

Skill Level
★★★ Challenging

Instructions
Rose Ring (make 12)
Rose No. 1

Rnd 1: With G hook and variegated, ch 7, sl st in first ch to form ring, ch 5, (dc in ring, ch 2) 7 times, join with sl st in 3rd ch of ch-5 (8 dc, 8 ch sps).

Rnd 2: Ch 1; for petals, (sc, ch 1, 3 dc, ch 1, sc) in each ch-2 sp around, **do not** join (8 petals).

Rnd 3: Working behind petals, sl st around post of first dc on rnd 1, ch 6, (dc around post of next dc on rnd 1, ch 3) around, join with sl st in 3rd ch of ch-6.

Rnd 4: Ch 1, (sc, ch 1, 5 dc, ch 1, sc) in each ch-3 sp around, **do not** join.

Rnd 5: Sl st around post of first dc on rnd 3, ch 7, (dc around post of next dc on rnd 3, ch 4) around, join with sl st in 3rd ch of ch-7.

Rnd 6: Ch 1, (sc, ch 1, 7 dc, ch 1, sc) in each ch-4 sp around, join with sl st in first sc, fasten off.

Rose No. 2
Rnds 1-5: Repeat same rnds of Rose No. 1.

Rnd 6: Ch 1, (sc, ch 1, 4 dc) in first ch sp, ch 1, sl st in 4th dc of one 7-dc petal on last Rose, ch 1, sl st in top of last dc made, (3 dc, ch 1, sc) in same sp on this Rose, (sc, ch 1, 7 dc, ch 1, sc) in each ch sp around, join with sl st in first sc, fasten off.

Roses No. 3-7
Rnds 1-5: Repeat same rnds of Rose No. 1.

Rnd 6: Ch 1, (sc, ch 1, 4 dc) in first ch sp, ch 1, sl st in 4th dc of corresponding 7-dc petal on last Rose (3 free petals on each side of joined petals), ch 1, sl st in top of last dc made, (3 dc, ch 1, sc) in same sp on this Rose, (sc, ch 1, 7 dc, ch 1, sc) in each ch sp around, join with sl st in first sc, fasten off.

Rose No. 8
Rnds 1-5: Repeat same rnds of Rose No. 1.

Rnd 6: Ch 1, (sc, ch 1, 4 dc) in first ch sp, ch 1, sl st in 4th dc of corresponding 7-dc petal on last Rose, ch 1, sl st in top of last dc made, (3 dc, ch 1, sc) in same sp on this Rose, (sc, ch 1, 7 dc, ch 1, sc) in each of next 3 ch sps, (sc, ch 1, 4 dc) in next ch sp, ch 1, sl st in 4th dc on corresponding petal of Rose No. 1, ch 1, sl st in top of last dc made, (3 dc, ch 1, sc) in same sp on this Rose, (sc, ch 1, 7 dc, ch 1, sc) in each of last 3 ch sps, join with sl st in first sc, fasten off.

Center Rose (make 12)
Rnd 1: With H hook and dk. rose, repeat same rnd of Rose No. 1.

Rnd 2: Ch 1; for petals, (sc, ch 1, dc, tr, dc, ch 1, sc) in each ch sp around, **do not** join (8 petals).

Continued on page 18

Sunburst

katherine eng, designer

Bright yellow sunflowers shine on a sky blue background. Bask in the golden warmth of a summer's day beneath this fresh and innovative throw.

Finished Size
44" x 65"

Materials
Worsted-weight yarn — 21 oz. med. blue, 13 oz. each dk. yellow and dk. blue, 4½ oz. orange and 3 oz. lt. yellow; tapestry needle; G crochet hook or size needed to obtain gauge.

Gauge
4 sts = 1"; 4 sc rows = 1".
Each Block is 7" square.

Skill Level
★★ Average

Instructions
Block (make 40)
Notes: For **beginning cluster (beg cl),** ch 4, *yo 2 times, insert hook in ring, yo, draw lp through, (yo, draw through 2 lps on hook) 2 times; repeat from *, yo, draw through all 3 lps on hook.

For **cluster (cl),** *yo 2 times, insert hook in ring, yo, draw lp through, (yo, draw through 2 lps on hook) 2 times; repeat from * 2 more times, yo, draw through all 4 lps on hook.

Rnd 1: With lt. yellow, ch 4, sl st in first ch to form ring, beg cl, ch 4, (cl, ch 4) 5 times, join with sl st in top of first cl, fasten off (6 cls).

Rnd 2: Join orange with sc in any ch sp, 5 sc in same sp, 6 sc in each ch sp around, join with sl st in first sc (36 sc).

Rnd 3: Ch 1, sc in each st around, join, fasten off.

Rnd 4: Join dk. yellow with sc in any st, sc in each st around, join.

Rnd 5: Ch 3, 2 dc in first st, skip next st, *(sl st, ch 3, 2 dc) in next st, skip next st; repeat from * around, join with sl st in joining sl st on last rnd.

Rnd 6: Sl st in next ch-3 sp, ch 1, sc in same sp, ch 3, (sc in next ch-3 sp, ch 3) around, join with sl st in first sc, fasten off (18 ch sps).

Rnd 7: Join med. blue with sc in ch sp above any cl on rnd 1, 2 sc in same sp, sc in next st, (3 sc in next ch sp, sc in next st) around, join (72 sc).

Rnd 8: Ch 1, sc in first 5 sts, *[hdc in each of next 2 sts, dc in each of next 2 sts, tr in each of next 2 sts, (2 tr, ch 3, 2 tr) in next st, tr in each of next 2 sts, dc in each of next 2 sts, hdc in each of next 2 sts], sc in next 5 sts; repeat from * 2 more times; repeat between [ ], join.

Rnd 9: Ch 1, sc in each st around with (2 sc, ch 2, 2 sc) in each corner ch sp, join, fasten off (100 sc, 4 ch sps).

Rnd 10: Join dk. blue with sc in any corner ch sp, ch 3, sc in same sp, *[ch 1, skip next st, (sc in next st, ch 1, skip next st) across to next corner ch sp], (sc, ch 3, sc) in next corner ch sp; repeat from * 2 more times; repeat between [ ], join, fasten off.

Holding Blocks wrong sides together, matching sts, working in **back lps** *(see fig. 1, pg. 158)* through both thicknesses, sew Blocks together in five rows of eight Blocks each.

Border
Rnd 1: With right side facing you, join dk. blue with sc in any corner ch sp, ch 3, sc in same sp, sc in each st, sc in each ch-1 sp, hdc

Continued on page 23

Flowers on Parade

jacqueline jewett, designer

Flowers, flowers everywhere! Bright ones, bold ones, all in a row, parade across this gorgeous afghan. Shades of pink, turquoise and purple complement each other and create a stunning effect.

Finished Size
43" x 60"

Materials
Worsted-weight yarn — 11½ oz. each dk. pink and green, 8 oz. each purple, turquoise, rose and off-white; F crochet hook or size needed to obtain gauge.

Gauge
5 dc sts = 1". Each Motif is 4¾" across from point to point.

Skill Level
★★ Average

Instructions
First Row
First Motif
Rnd 1: With off-white, ch 6, sl st in first ch to form ring, ch 1, 12 sc in ring, join with sl st in first sc (12 sc).

Rnd 2: Ch 3, dc in same st, 2 dc in each st around, join with sl st in top of ch-3, fasten off (24 dc).

Rnd 3: Join turquoise with sl st in any st, ch 3, dc in each of next 2 sts, ch 3, (dc in each of next 3 sts, ch 3) 7 times, join, **turn** (8 ch sps).

Note: For **shell,** (2 dc, 3 tr, 2 dc) in next ch sp.

Rnd 4: Sl st in next ch sp, ch 3, (dc, 3 tr, 2 dc) in same sp, shell in each ch sp around, join, **turn,** fasten off.

Rnd 5: Join dk. pink with sc in first st of any shell, sc in each st around with (sc, ch 3, sc) in center st of each shell, join with sl st in first sc, fasten off.

Second Motif
Rnds 1-4: With colors indicated on Motif Diagram (pg. 15), repeat same rnds of First Motif.

Rnd 5: Join indicated color with sc in first st of any shell, sc in each of next 3 sts, ch 1; working in side of last Motif, sc in corresponding ch-3 sp, ch 1, sc in same st as last sc on this Motif, sc in next 7 sts, ch 1, sc in next ch-3 sp on other Motif, ch 1, sc in same st as last sc on this Motif, sc in each st around with (sc, ch 3, sc) in center st of each shell, join with sl st in first sc, fasten off.

Repeat Second Motif seven more times for a total of nine Motifs.

Second Row
First Motif
Joining to bottom of First Row First Motif, work same as First Row Second Motif.

Second Motif
Rnds 1-4: With colors indicated, repeat same rnds of First Row First Motif.

Rnd 5: Join indicated color with sc in first st of any shell, sc in each of next 3 sts, ch 1; working on bottom of next Motif on row above, (sc in corresponding ch-3 sp on other Motif, ch 1, sc in same st as last sc on this Motif, sc in next 7 sts, ch 1, sc in next ch-3 sp on other Motif, ch 1, sc in same st as last sc on this Motif), sc in next 7 sts; working on side of last Motif on this row; repeat between ( ), sc in each st around with (sc, ch 3, sc) in center st of each shell, join with sl st in first sc, fasten off.

Repeat Second Motif seven more times for a total of nine Motifs.

Next Rows
Repeat Second Row 11 more times for a total of 13 rows.

Continued on page 14

Flowers on Parade

Continued from page 13

Motif Insertion

Working in open area between joining of Motifs, join green with sl st in 2nd sc after any joining, ch 3, dc in next 5 sts; *working on next Motif, dc in 2nd sc past next joining, dc in next 5 sts; repeat from * 2 more times, join with sl st in top of ch-3, fasten off.

Repeat in each open area between Motifs.

Border

Notes: For **beginning cluster (beg cl),** ch 3, (yo, insert hook in same ch sp, yo, draw lp through, yo, draw through 2 lps on hook) 2 times, yo, draw through all 3 lps on hook.

For **cluster (cl),** yo, insert hook in next ch sp, yo, draw lp through, yo, draw through 2 lps on hook, (yo, insert hook in same ch sp, yo, draw lp through, yo, draw through 2 lps on hook) 2 times, yo, draw through all 4 lps on hook.

Rnd 1: Join green with sl st in first ch-3 sp on top right-hand Motif, beg cl, (ch 3, dc in each of next 3 sts, skip next 2 sts, dc in each of next 3 sts, ch 3, cl in next ch sp) 3 times, *[dc in each of next 3 sts, skip next 2 sts, dc in each of next 3 sts, skip next joining, dc in each of next 3 sts, skip next 2 sts, dc in each of next 3 sts, ch 3], cl in next ch sp; repeat between ( )*; repeat between ** 7 more times; repeat between ( ) 2 more times; repeat between ** 12 more times; repeat between ( ) 2 more times; repeat between ** 8 more times; repeat between ( ) 2 more times; repeat between ** 11 more times; repeat between [ ], join with sl st in first cl, fasten off.

Rnd 2: Join dk. pink with sl st in first cl, beg cl in same cl, (ch 3, dc in next ch sp, dc in each of next 2 sts, skip next 2 sts, dc in each of next 2 sts, dc in next ch sp, ch 3, cl in next cl) 3 times, *[ch 3, dc in next ch sp, dc in next 5 sts, skip next 2 sts, dc in next 5 sts, dc in next ch sp, ch 3], cl in next cl; repeat between ( )*; repeat between ** 7 more times; repeat between ( ) 2 more times; repeat between ** 12 more times; repeat between ( ) 2 more times; repeat between ** 8 more times; repeat between ( ) 2 more times; repeat between ** 11 more times; repeat between [ ], join with sl st in first cl, fasten off.❖

First
Motif

Second
Motif

MOTIF DIAGRAM

First
Row

Second
Row

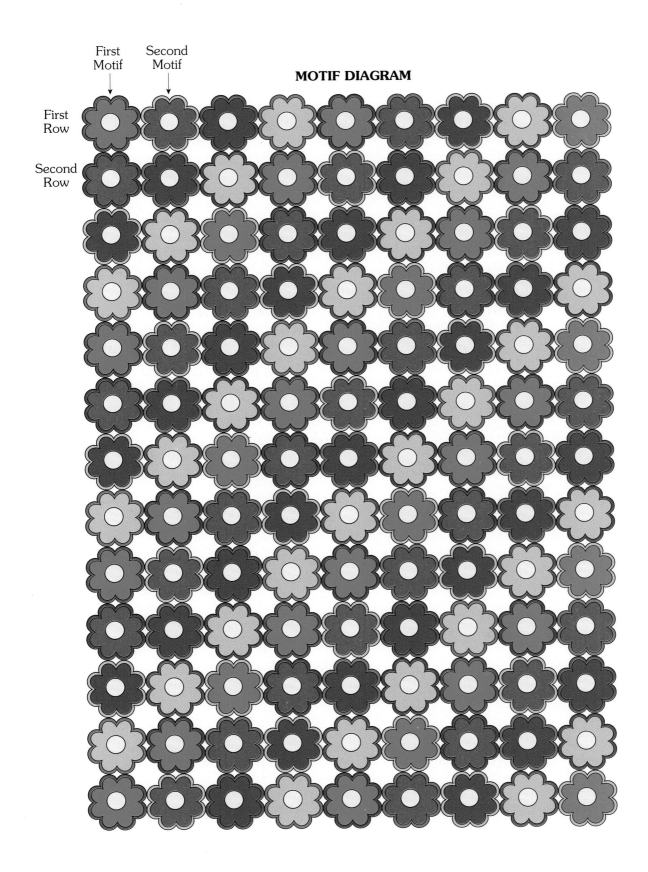

Spring Fever

ruth owens, designer

Softly blushing innocent pink blossoms nestled amid gentle waves of spring's first greens evoke feelings of renewal and gratitude for the season's glorious rebirth.

Finished Size
46" x 71"

Materials
Worsted-weight yarn — 25 oz. white, 11 oz. lt. pink, 7 oz. each lt. green, med. green and dk. green; I crochet hook or size needed to obtain gauge.

Gauge
3 dc sts = 1"; 3 dc rows = 2".

Skill Level
★★ Average

Instructions

Afghan

Row 1: With white, ch 180, 2 dc in 4th ch from hook, (*dc in next 5 chs , yo, insert hook in next ch, yo, draw lp through, yo, draw through 2 lps on hook, skip next 3 chs, yo, insert hook in next ch, yo, draw lp through, yo, draw through 2 lps on hook, yo, draw through all 3 lps on hook, dc in next 5 chs*, 5 dc in next ch) 10 times; repeat between **, 3 dc in last ch, turn, fasten off (177 dc).

Notes: For **treble horizontal cluster (tr hcl),** ch 4, *yo 2 times, insert hook in top of last st made, yo, draw lp through, (yo, draw through 2 lps on hook) 2 times; repeat from * 2 more times, yo, draw through all 4 lps on hook.

For **treble cluster (tr cl),** yo 2 times, insert hook in next st, yo, draw lp through, (yo, draw through 2 lps on hook) 2 times, *yo 2 times, insert hook in same st, yo, draw lp through, (yo, draw through 2 lps on hook) 2 times; repeat from * 2 more times, yo, draw through all 5 lps on hook.

Row 2: Join lt. pink with sc in first st, sc in same st, (*sc in each of next 2 sts, tr hcl, skip next 5 sts, tr cl in next st, tr hcl, skip next 5 sts, sc in each of next 2 sts*, 3 sc in next st) 10 times; repeat between **, 2 sc in last st, turn.

Row 3: Ch 1, sc in first st, (ch 7, skip next 3 sc and next tr hcl, tr cl in next tr cl, ch 7, skip next tr hcl and 3 sc, sc in next sc) across, turn, fasten off.

Row 4: Join white with sl st in first st, ch 3, 5 dc in next ch sp, (5 dc in next tr cl, 5 dc in next ch sp, dc same ch sp and next ch sp tog, 5 dc in same ch sp as last half of last dc) 10 times, 5 dc in next tr cl, 5 dc in next ch sp, dc same ch sp and last st tog, turn, fasten off (177 dc).

Notes: For **beginning dc cluster (beg dc cl),** ch 3, (yo, insert hook in same st, yo, draw lp through, yo, draw through 2 lps on hook) 2 times, yo, draw through all 3 lps on hook.

For **dc cluster (dc cl),** yo, insert hook in next st, yo, draw lp through, yo, draw through 2 lps on hook, (yo, insert hook in same st, yo, draw lp through, yo, draw through 2 lps on hook) 2 times, yo, draw through all 4 lps on hook.

Row 5: Join lt. green with sl st in first st, beg dc cl, (skip next 2 sts, dc in next 5 sts, 5 dc in next st, dc in next 5 sts, skip next 2 sts, dc cl in next st) across, turn, fasten off.

Rows 6-10: Working in color sequence of white, med. green, white, dk. green, white, repeat row 5.

Continued on page 18

Spring Fever

Continued from page 16

Note: For **beginning treble cluster (beg tr cl),** ch 4, *yo 2 times, insert hook in same st, yo, draw lp through, (yo, draw through 2 lps on hook) 2 times; repeat from * 2 more times, yo, draw through all 4 lps on hook.

Row 11: Join lt. pink with sl st in first st, beg tr cl, tr hcl, (*skip next 5 sts, sc in each of next 2 sts, 3 sc in next st, sc in each of next 2 sts, tr hcl, skip next 5 sts, tr cl in next cl*, tr hcl) 10 times; repeat between **, turn.

Row 12: Beg tr cl, (ch 7, skip next tr hcl and next 3 sc, sc in next st, ch 7, skip next 3 sc and next tr hcl, tr cl in next tr cl) across, turn, fasten off.

Row 13: Join white with sl st in first st, ch 3, 2 dc in same st, (*5 dc in next ch sp, dc same ch sp and next ch sp tog, 5 dc in same ch sp as last half of last dc*, 5 dc in next tr cl) 10 times; repeat between **, 3 dc in last tr cl, turn, fasten off.

Row 14: Join dk. green with sl st in first st, ch 3, 2 dc in same st, (*dc in next 5 sts, skip next 2 sts, dc cl in next st, skip next 2 sts, dc in next 5 sts*, 5 dc in next st) 10 times; repeat between **, 3 dc in last st, turn, fasten off.

Rows 15-19: Working in color sequence of white, med. green, white, lt. green, white, repeat row 14.

Rows 20-82: Repeat rows 2-19 consecutively, ending with row 10.

Row 83: Working in starting ch on opposite side of row 1, with wrong side of row 1 facing you, join lt. green with sl st in first ch, beg dc cl, (skip next ch, dc in next 5 chs, 5 dc in next ch sp, dc in next 5 chs, skip next ch, dc cl in next ch) across, turn, fasten off.

Rows 84-88: Working in color sequence of white, med. green, white, dk. green, white, repeat row 5.✳

Cabbage Roses

Continued from page 9

Rnd 3: Sl st around post of first dc on rnd 1, ch 7, (tr around post of next dc on rnd 1, ch 3) around, join with sl st in 4th ch of ch-7.

Rnd 4: Ch 1, (sc, ch 1, dc, 3 tr, dc, ch 1, sc) in each ch sp around, **do not** join.

Rnd 5: Sl st around post of first tr on rnd 3, ch 8, (tr around post of next tr on rnd 3, ch 4) around, join with sl st in 4th ch of ch-8.

Rnd 6: Ch 1, (sc, ch 1, dc, 5 tr, dc, ch 1, sc) in each ch sp around, join with sl st in first sc, fasten off.

Block (make 12)

Rnd 1: Holding one Center Rose in center of one Rose Ring, with H hook and off-white, join with sl st in 2nd tr of any petal on rnd 6 of Center Rose, ch 6, sl st in 4th dc of center free petal on rnd 6 of any Rose on Rose Ring, ch 6, skip next tr on Center Rose, sl st in next tr, (ch 6, sl st in 2nd tr of next petal on Center Rose, ch 6, sl st in 4th dc on center free petal of next Rose on Rose Ring, ch 6, skip next tr on Center Rose, sl st in next tr) around, ch 6, join with sl st in first sl st, fasten off.

Row 2: Working in rows, in open areas between Rose Ring and rnd 1, join off-white with sl st in 5th ch of 2nd ch-6 (see Block Diagram), ch 2, (3 dc, ch 3, 3 dc) in next ch-6 sp, ch 2, sl st in 2nd ch of next ch-6, turn.

Row 3: Sl st in next ch-2 sp, ch 3, sl st in joined st on center petal of corresponding Rose on Rose Ring, (2 dc, ch 3, 3 dc) in same ch sp on this row, (3 dc, ch 3, 3 dc) in next ch-3 sp, (3 dc, ch 3, 3 dc) in next ch-2 sp, sl st in joined st on center petal of next Rose on Rose Ring, turn.

Row 4: Sl st in each of next 3 dc, sl st in next ch-3 sp, ch 2, sl st in 4th dc on next free petal on Rose Ring, ch 2, 3 dc in next ch-3 sp, ch 3, sl st in next joining between Roses on Rose Ring, ch 3, 3 dc in same ch-3 sp on this row, ch 2, sl st in 4th dc of next free petal on Rose Ring, ch 2, sl st in next ch-3 sp on this row, fasten off.

Joining in next free ch-6 on rnd 1, repeat rows 2-4 seven more times.

Rnd 5: Working around outside edge of Rose Ring, join off-white with sc in 4th dc of center free petal on any Rose, [ch 3, sc in same st, *◊ch 2, dc in first sc on next petal, ch 2, sc in 4th dc of same petal, ch 2, tr in first sc of next petal, ch 2, tr in 3rd dc of same petal, ch 2, tr in next joining, ch 2, tr in next dc on next petal, ch 2, tr in first sc on next petal, ch 2, sc in 4th dc on same petal, ch 2, dc in first sc on next petal, ch 2◊, sc in 4th dc of same petal*]; repeat between **; repeat between [ ]; repeat between **; repeat between [ ]; repeat between **; repeat between [ ]; repeat between ◊◊, join with sl st in first sc.

Rnd 6: Sl st in next ch-3 sp, ch 3, (2 dc, ch 3, 3 dc) in same sp, *[(ch 3, sc in next ch-2 sp) 4 times, (dc in next tr, dc in next ch sp) 2 times, dc in next tr, (sc in next ch-2 sp, ch 3) 7 times, sc in next ch-2 sp, (dc in next tr, dc in next ch-2 sp) 2 times, dc in next tr, (sc in next ch-2 sp, ch 3) 4 times], (3 dc, ch 3, 3 dc) in next ch-3 sp; repeat from * 2 more times; repeat between [ ], join with sl st in top of ch-3.

Rnd 7: Ch 3, dc in each of next 2 sts, *[(3 dc, ch 3, 3 dc) in next ch sp, dc in each of next 3 sts, (dc in next ch sp, dc in next st) 3 times, dc in next ch sp, skip next sc, (tr in next st, skip next st) 3 times, hdc in next ch sp, hdc in next sc, (sc in next ch sp, sc in next st) 4 times, sc in next ch sp, hdc in next st, hdc in next ch sp, skip next sc, (tr in next st, skip next st) 3 times, (dc in next ch sp, dc in next st) 3 times, dc in next ch sp], dc in each of next 3 sts; repeat from * 2 more

times; repeat between [ ], join.

Rnd 8: Ch 3, dc in next 5 sts, *[(3 dc, ch 3, 3 dc) in next ch sp, dc in next 6 sts, tr in next 12 sts, dc in next st, hdc in next st, sc in next 5 sts, hdc in next st, dc in next st, tr in next 12 sts], dc in next 6 sts; repeat from * 2 more times; repeat between [ ], join.

Rnd 9: Ch 3, dc in each st around with (3 dc, ch 3, 3 dc) in each corner ch sp, join, fasten off.

Holding Blocks wrong sides together, matching sts, working in **back lps** *(see fig. 1, pg. 158)* through both thicknesses, sew together with off-white in three rows of four Blocks each.

Border
Rnd 1: Join dk. rose with sl st in any corner ch-3 sp on one short end, (ch 3, 2 dc, ch 3, 3 dc) in same sp, dc in each st and 2 dc in each ch sp before and after seams around with (3 dc, ch 3, 3 dc) in each corner ch sp, join with sl st in top of ch-3 (185 sts on each short end, 246 sts on each long edge, 4 ch-3 sps).

Rnd 2: Sl st in each of next 2 sts, (sl st, ch 3, 2 dc, ch 3, 3 dc) in next ch sp, *[sc in next st, (dc in next st, tr in next st, dc in next st, sc in next st) across] to next ch sp, (3 dc, ch 3, 3 dc) in next ch sp*, skip next st; repeat between ** 2 more times, skip next st; repeat between [ ], join, fasten off.✦

Block Diagram

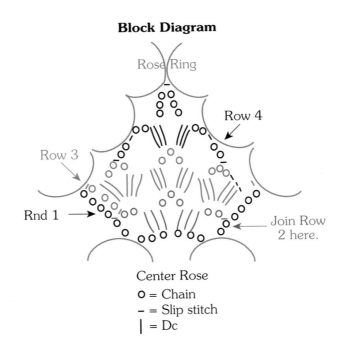

Rose Ring

Row 4

Row 3

Rnd 1

Join Row 2 here.

Center Rose

o = Chain
– = Slip stitch
| = Dc

Perennial Medley

katherine eng, designer

Spring is running rampant on this brightly flowered blanket. As you gaze at the colorful blossoms, you can almost smell the sweet perfume of a perfect spring day.

Finished Size
44" x 50"

Materials
Worsted-weight yarn — 36 oz. navy, 12 oz. med. blue, 4 oz. each yellow, lavender, lt. blue, pink, green and coral; tapestry needle; H crochet hook or size needed to obtain gauge.

Gauge
7 sc sts = 2"; 7 sc rows = 2". Each Block is 7½" square.

Skill Level
★★ Average

Instructions
Block No. 1 (make 6)
Rnd 1: With green, ch 4, sl st in first ch to form ring, ch 1, 8 sc in ring, join with sl st in first sc (8 sc).

Rnd 2: Ch 1, sc in first st, 2 sc in next st, (sc in next st, 2 sc in next st) around, join, fasten off (12).

Rnd 3: Join lavender with sc in first st, 5 dc in next st, (sc in next st, 5 dc in next st) around, join.

Rnd 4: Ch 1, sc in first st, (ch 4; working behind dc, sc in next sc) 5 times, ch 4, join.

Rnd 5: Skipping sc and working in dc on rnd 3, ch 1, (sc in each of next 2 dc, 3 sc in next dc, sc in each of next 2 dc) around, join.

Rnd 6: Ch 1, sc in each of first 2 sts, (hdc in next st; for **petal**, 5 dc in next st; hdc in next st, sc in next 4 sts) 5 times, hdc in next st; for **petal**, 5 dc in next st; hdc in next st, sc in each of last 2 sts, join (6 petals).

Rnd 7: Sl st in next st, *[ch 2, skip next st, sl st in next st, ch 2, skip next st, (sl st, ch 2, sl st) in next st, (ch 2, skip next st, sl st in next st) 2 times], sl st in each of next 3 sts; repeat from * 4 more times; repeat between [ ], sl st in last st, join with sl st in joining sl st on last rnd, fasten off.

Rnd 8: Join navy with sl st in any skipped sc of rnd 4, ch 3, 5 dc in next ch sp, (dc in next skipped sc, 5 dc in next ch sp) around, join with sl st in top of ch-3 (36 dc).

Rnd 9: Ch 3, 4 dc in first st, (*dc in next st, hdc in next st, sc in next 4 sts, hdc in next st, dc in next st*, 5 dc in next st) 3 times; repeat between **, join.

Rnd 10: Ch 1, sc in each st around with (sc, ch 2, sc) in center dc of each 5-dc group, join with sl st in first sc, **turn** (56 sc, 4 ch sps).

Rnd 11: Ch 1, sc in next st and ch-2 sp at tip of corresponding petal at same time, sc in each of next 2 sts, *sc next 2 sts tog, sc in each of next 3 sts, sc in next st and ch-2 sp at tip of next petal at same time, sc in each of next 2 sts, (sc, ch 2, sc) in next ch sp, sc in next 6 sts, sc next 2 sts tog, sc in next 6 sts, (sc, ch 2, sc) in next ch sp*, sc in each of next 2 sts, sc in next st and ch-2 sp at tip of next corresponding petal at same time, sc in each of next 3 sts; repeat between **, sc in each of last 3 sts, join, **turn.**

Rnd 12: Ch 1, *sc in each st across to next corner ch sp, (sc, ch 2, sc) in next corner ch sp, sc in next 7 sts, sc in next st and ch-2 at tip of corresponding petal at same time, sc in each st across to next corner ch sp, (sc, ch 2, sc) in next corner ch sp; repeat from *, sc in each st across, join, **turn.**

Continued on page 22

Continued from page 20

Rnd 13: Ch 1, sc in each st around with (sc, ch 2, sc) in each corner ch sp, join, **turn.**

Rnd 14: Repeat rnd 13, **do not** turn, fasten off.

Note: For **long single crochet (lsc),** working over sts of last rnd, insert hook in next st on rnd before last, draw up long lp same height as last st on rnd being worked, yo, draw through both lps on hook. Skip st on last row behind lsc.

Rnd 15: Join med. blue with sc in any corner ch sp, ch 2, sc in same sp, *sc in next st, (lsc, sc in next st) across to next corner ch sp, (sc, ch 2, sc) in next corner ch sp; repeat from * 2 more times, sc in next st, (lsc, sc in next st) across, join, fasten off.

Rnd 16: Join navy with sc in any corner ch sp, ch 3, sc in same sp, *[ch 1, skip next st, (sc in next st, ch 1, skip next st) across] to next corner ch sp, (sc, ch 3, sc) in next corner ch sp; repeat from * 2 more times; repeat between [ ], join, fasten off.

Block No. 2 (make 6)

Substituting lt. blue for green and coral for lavender, work same as Block No. 1.

Block No. 3 (make 6)

Substituting yellow for green and pink for lavender, work same as Block No. 1.

Block No. 4 (make 6)

Substituting coral for green and lt. blue for lavender, work same as Block No. 1.

Block No. 5 (make 6)

Substituting lavender for green and green for lavender, work same as Block No. 1.

Block No. 6 (make 5)

Substituting pink for green and yellow for lavender, work same as Block No. 1.

Assembly

With tapestry needle and navy, working in **back lps** *(see fig. 1, pg. 158)* only, sew Blocks together in five rows of seven Blocks each according to Assembly Diagram.

Border

Rnd 1: With wrong side facing you, join navy with sc in any st on one long edge, sc in each st, sc in each ch-1 sp, hdc in each ch sp on each side of seams and hdc in each seam around with (sc, ch 3, sc) in each corner ch sp, join with sl st in first sc, **turn** (139 sts on each short end, 195 sts on each long edge, 4 ch sps).

Rnd 2: Ch 1, sc in each st around with (sc, ch 3, sc) in each corner ch sp, join, **do not** turn, fasten off.

Rnd 3: Join med. blue with sc in any corner ch sp, ch 3, sc in same sp, *[ch 1, skip next st, (sc in next st, ch 1, skip next st) across] to next corner ch sp, (sc, ch 3, sc) in next corner ch sp; repeat from * 2 more times; repeat between [ ], join, **turn.**

Rnd 4: Sl st in next ch sp, ch 1, sc in same sp, *ch 1, (sc in next ch sp, ch 1) across to next corner ch sp, (sc, ch 3, sc) in next corner ch sp; repeat from * 3 more times, ch 1, join, **turn,** fasten off.

Rnd 5: Join navy with sc in any corner ch sp, ch 3, sc in same sp, *ch 1, (sc in next ch sp, ch 1) across to next corner ch sp, (sc, ch 3, sc) in next corner ch sp; repeat from * 2 more times, ch 1, (sc in next ch sp, ch 1) across, join, **do not** turn.

Rnd 6: Ch 1, sc in each st and in each ch-1 sp around with (sc, ch 3, sc) in each corner ch sp, join, **turn.**

Rnd 7: Ch 1, sc in each st around with (sc, ch 3, sc) in each corner ch sp, join, **do not** turn.

Rnd 8: Sl st in next st, ch 1, sc in same st, *ch 1, skip next st, (sc in next st, ch 1, skip next st) across to next corner ch sp, (sc, ch 3, sc) in next corner ch sp; repeat from * 3 more times, ch 1, skip next st, sc in next st, ch 1, skip next st, join, **turn.**

Rnd 9: (Sl st, ch 1, sc, ch 2, sc) in next ch-1 sp, (sc, ch 2, sc) in each ch-1 sp around with

ASSEMBLY DIAGRAM

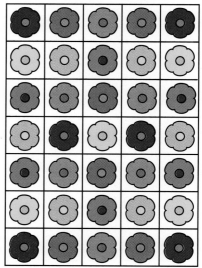

(sc, ch 3, sc) in each corner ch-3 sp, join, **do not** turn, fasten off.

Rnd 10: Join med. blue with sl st in 2nd ch-2 sp after any corner ch sp, ch 2, (sl st, ch 2) in each ch-2 sp around with (sl st, ch 3, sl st, ch 2) in each corner ch sp, join with sl st in first sl st.

Rnd 11: Ch 1, *sc in next ch-2 sp, (4 dc in next ch-2 sp, sc in next ch-2 sp) across to next corner ch sp, 6 dc in next corner ch sp; repeat from * 3 more times, sc in next ch sp,

4 dc in last ch sp, join with sl st in first sc.

Rnd 12: *(Ch 1, skip next dc, sl st in next dc, ch 3, sl st in next dc, ch 1, skip next dc, sl st in next sc) across to next corner, ch 2, skip next dc, sl st in next dc, ch 2, sl st in next dc, ch 3, sl st in next dc, ch 2, sl st in next dc, ch 2, skip next dc, sl st in next sc; repeat from * 3 more times, ch 1, skip next dc, sl st in next dc, ch 3, sl st in next dc, ch 1, skip next dc, join with sl st in joining sl st of last rnd, fasten off.✤

Sunburst

Continued from page 10

in each ch sp on each side of seams and hdc in each seam around with (sc, ch 3, sc) in each corner ch sp, join with sl st in first sc, **turn** (149 sts on each short end, 239 sts on each long edge, 4 ch sps).

Rnd 2: Sl st in next st, ch 1, sc in same st, *ch 1, skip next st, (sc in next st, ch 1, skip next st) across to next corner ch sp, (sc, ch 3, sc) in next corner ch sp; repeat from * 3 more times, ch 1, join, **turn,** fasten off.

Rnd 3: Join med. blue with sl st in any corner ch sp, ch 3, (dc, ch 2, 2 dc) in same sp, dc in each st and in each ch-1 sp around with (2 dc, ch 2, 2 dc) in each corner ch sp, join with sl st in top of ch-3, **turn.**

Rnd 4: Ch 1, sc in first st, *ch 1, skip next st, (sc in next st, ch 1, skip next st) across to next corner ch sp, (sc, ch 3, sc) in corner ch sp; repeat from * 3 more times, ch 1, join with sl st in first sc, **turn.**

Rnd 5: Ch 1, sc in each st and in each ch-1 sp around with (sc, ch 3, sc) in each corner ch sp, join, **do not** turn, fasten off.

Rnd 6: Join dk. yellow with sc in any corner ch sp, ch 3, sc in same sp, *[ch 1, skip next st, (sc in next st, ch 2, skip next 2 sts) across to 2 sts before next corner ch sp, sc in next st, ch 1, skip next st], (sc, ch 3, sc) in next corner ch sp; repeat from * 2 more times; repeat between [ ], join.

Rnd 7: Sl st in next ch sp, ch 3, 2 dc in same sp, (sl st, ch 3, 2 dc) in each st and in each corner ch sp around, join with sl st in joining sl st of last rnd.

Rnd 8: Sl st in next ch-3 sp, ch 1, (sc, ch 3, sc) in same sp, *ch 2, (sc in next ch-3 sp, ch 2) across to next corner ch sp, (sc, ch 3, sc) in

next corner ch sp; repeat from * 2 more times, ch 2, (sc in next ch-3 sp, ch 2) across, join with sl st in first sc, fasten off.

Rnd 9: Join med. blue with sc in any corner ch sp, ch 3, sc in same sp, 2 sc in each ch-2 sp and sc in each sc around with (sc, ch 3, sc) in each corner ch sp, join, **turn.**

Rnd 10: Repeat rnd 2, **do not** fasten off.

Rnd 11: Ch 3, dc in each st and in each ch-1 sp around with (2 dc, ch 2, 2 dc) in each corner ch sp, join with sl st in top of ch-3, fasten off.

Rnd 12: With dk. blue, repeat rnd 6.

Rnd 13: Ch 1, sc in first sc, *5 dc in next corner ch sp, sc in next sc, (5 dc in next sc, sc in next sc) across to next corner ch sp; repeat from * 2 more times, 5 dc in next corner ch sp, (sc in next sc, 5 dc in next sc) across, join.

Rnd 14: Ch 1, sc in first st, [ch 2, skip next 2 dc, (sc, ch 3, sc, ch 3, sc) in next dc, ch 2, sc in next sc, *ch 2, (sc, ch 3, sc) in center dc of next 5-dc group, ch 2, sc in next sc; repeat from * across to next corner 5-dc group]; repeat between [ ] 2 more times, ch 2, skip next 2 dc, (sc, ch 3, sc, ch 3, sc) in next dc, ch 2, ◊sc in next sc, ch 2, (sc, ch 3, sc) in center dc of next 5-dc group, ch 2; repeat from ◊ across, join.

Note: For **shell,** (sl st, ch 3, sl st) in next ch sp.

Rnd 15: *[Ch 3, skip next ch sp, shell in next ch sp, ch 5, shell in next ch sp, ch 3, skip next ch sp], sl st in next sc, (ch 3, skip next ch sp, shell in next ch sp, ch 3, skip next ch sp, sl st in next sc) across to next corner; repeat from * 2 more times; repeat between [ ], (sl st in next sc, ch 3, skip next ch sp, shell in next ch sp, ch 3) across, join with sl st in joining sl st of last rnd, fasten off.✤

Lavish Lace

Sumptuous blends of stitches and loops embellish a fanciful profusion
of delicate, graceful creations suitable for the most discriminating
connoisseur. Convey a sense of peaceful elegance in your
private retreat through a tasteful collection
of crochet confections.

Crystal Lace

roberta maier, designer

As breathtakingly beautiful as fine crystal, this lusciously textured cover recalls a more gentle time. Filigreed strips make its reproduction a pleasant task.

Finished Size
46" x 72"

Materials
Worsted-weight yarn — 37 oz. white and 14 oz. blue; H crochet hook or size needed to obtain gauge.

Gauge
1 shell = 1¼"; 8 shell rows = 5".

Skill Level
★★ Average

Instructions

Strip (make 8)

Note: For **cluster (cl),** ch 4, yo, insert hook in 4th ch from hook, yo, draw lp through, yo, draw through 2 lps on hook, yo, insert hook in same ch, yo, draw lp through, yo, draw through 2 lps on hook, yo, draw through all 3 loops on hook.

Row 1: With white, ch 19, 2 dc in 4th ch from hook, ch 2, 2 dc in next ch, cl, skip next 5 chs, sc in next ch, cl, skip next 5 chs, 2 dc in next ch, ch 2, 2 dc in next ch, dc in last ch, turn (10 dc, 2 cl, 2 ch sps, 1 sc).

Note: For **shell,** (2 dc, ch 2, 2 dc) in next ch sp.

Row 2: Ch 3, shell in next ch sp, ch 2, skip next cl, (dc, ch 3, dc) in next sc, ch 2, skip next cl, shell in next ch sp, dc in last st, turn (4 dc, 2 shells).

Row 3: Ch 3, shell in ch sp of next shell, cl, skip next ch-2 sp, sc in next ch-3 sp, cl, shell in ch sp of next shell, dc in last st, turn.

Rows 4-111: Repeat rows 2 and 3 alternately.

Row 112: Ch 1, sc in first st, skip next dc on next shell, sc in next dc, sc in next ch-2 sp, ch 5, skip next cl, sc in next sc, ch 5, skip next cl, sc in ch sp of next shell, sc in next dc on same shell, skip next dc, sc in last st, turn, fasten off (7 sc, 2 ch-5 sps).

Rnd 113: Working around outer edge, join blue with sl st in end of row 1, ch 3, dc in same row, 2 dc in end of each row across to last row, 3 sc in next sc, 7 tr in next ch-5 sp; for **picot,** ch 7, sl st in top of last st made; 7 tr in next ch-5 sp, skip next 2 sts, 3 sc in last st, 2 dc in end of each row across; working on opposite side of starting ch, 3 sc in first ch, 7 tr in next ch-5 sp, picot, 7 tr in next ch-5 sp, 3 sc in last ch, join with sl st in top of ch-3, fasten off.

To **join Strips,** holding two Strips wrong sides together, matching sts, working through both thicknesses in **back lps** *(see fig. 1, pg. 158),* join blue with sl st in first dc on one side, (ch 1, sl st in next dc) across leaving tr and sc sts unworked at each end, fasten off.✿

Touch of Burgundy

roberta maier, designer

*Lacy white granny squares
with a splash of burgundy
create an elegant pattern
in this exquisite afghan.
Its simple beauty will add
grace and style to your decor.*

Finished Size
46" x 68"

Materials
Worsted-weight yarn — 45 oz. white and 10 oz. burgundy; G crochet hook or size needed to obtain gauge.

Gauge
Each Motif is 5½" square.

Skill Level
★★ Average

Instructions
Motif No. 1
Rnd 1: With white, ch 10, sl st in first ch to form ring, ch 4, 5 tr in ring, ch 3, (6 tr in ring, ch 3) 3 times, join with sl st in top of ch-4, fasten off (24 tr, 4 ch sps).

Rnd 2: Working in spaces between sts, join burgundy with sl st in sp between first and 2nd sts, ch 4, tr in next 4 sps, ch 5, sc in next ch sp, ch 5, (tr in next 5 sps, ch 5, sc in next ch sp, ch 5) around, join, fasten off (20 tr, 8 ch sps, 4 sc).

Rnd 3: Join white with sc in first st, sc in next 4 sts, *[2 tr in next ch sp, (tr, ch 3, tr) in next sc, 2 tr in next ch sp], sc in next 5 sts; repeat from * 2 more times; repeat between [ ], join with sl st in first sc.

Rnd 4: Ch 1, sc in each st around with (sc, ch 3, sc) in each corner ch sp, join (52 sc, 4 ch sps).

Rnd 5: (Sl st, ch 1, sc) in next st, *[ch 5, skip next st, (sc in next st, ch 5, skip next st) across] to next corner ch sp, (sc, ch 7, sc) in next ch sp; repeat from * 3 more times; repeat between [ ], join, fasten off.

Motif No. 2
Rnds 1-4: Repeat same rnds of Motif No. 1.

Rnd 5: (Sl st, ch 1, sc) in next st, ch 5, skip next st, (sc in next st, ch 5, skip next st) across to next corner ch sp; holding Motifs wrong sides tog, to **join,** *sc in next corner ch sp, ch 3, sl st in center ch of corresponding ch-7 on last Motif, ch 3, sc in same sp on this Motif*, (ch 2, sl st in center ch of next ch-5 on other Motif, ch 2, skip next st on this Motif, sc in next st) 6 times, ch 2, sl st in center ch of next ch-5 on other Motif, ch 2, skip next sc on this Motif; repeat between **, [ch 5, skip next st, (sc in next st, ch 5, skip next st) across to next corner ch sp, (sc, ch 7, sc) in next corner ch sp]; repeat between [ ], ch 5, skip next st, (sc in next st, ch 5, skip next st) 2 times, join, fasten off.

Motifs No. 3-96
Joining Motifs in eight rows of twelve Motifs each, work same as Motif No 2.

Border
Rnd 1: Join white with sc in 3rd ch of ch-5 after any corner ch sp, *ch 5, (sc in 3rd ch of next ch-5 or in next joining, ch 5) across to next corner ch sp, (sc, ch 7, sc) in next corner ch sp; repeat from * 3 more times, ch 5, join with sl st in first sc.

Rnd 2: Sl st in each of next 2 chs, ch 1, sc in next ch, *ch 5, (sc in 3rd ch of next ch-5, ch 5) across to next corner ch sp, (sc, ch 7, sc) in next corner ch sp; repeat from * 3 more times, ch 5, sc in 3rd ch of next ch-5, ch 5, join, fasten off.✣

Peach Parfait

sandra miller-maxfield, designer

Dress up your favorite room with an unforgettable throw, handsomely crafted in velvety peach. Old-fashioned tassels are the perfect complement to this one-of-a-kind design.

Finished Size
53" x 66"

Materials
Worsted-weight yarn — 65 oz. peach; tapestry needle; H crochet hook or size needed to obtain gauge.

Gauge
7 dc sts = 2"; 2 dc rows and 1 sc row = 1½".

Skill Level
★★ Average

Instructions
Strip (make 12)
Note: For **puff st**, yo, insert hook in next ch or st, yo, draw up ½"-long lp, (yo, insert hook in same ch or st, yo, draw up ½"-long lp) 2 times, yo, draw through all 7 lps on hook.

Row 1: Ch 268, dc in 6th ch from hook, puff st in next ch, (ch 2, skip next 2 chs, dc in next ch, puff st in next ch) across to last ch, dc in last ch, ch 5, sl st in ch at base of last dc, **do not** turn (66 puff sts, 67 dc).

Rnd 2: Working in rnds, ch 1, sc in ch at base of next puff st; (for **spike,** ch 5, sc in 2nd ch from hook, hdc in next ch, dc in each of last 2 chs; sc in ch at base of next puff st) across; holding beginning ch-5 on row 1 to back, (spike, sc in top of next puff st) across; holding last ch-5 to back, spike, join with sl st in first sc.

Rnd 3: Working behind spikes, ch 1, 3 sc in each ch-2 sp between sts on row 1 around with 6 sc in each ch-5 sp, join (402 sc).

Rnd 4: Ch 3, dc in each st around with 2 dc in each of 6 sc on each end, join with sl st in top of ch-3 (414 dc).

Rnd 5: Ch 1, *sc in each st across to 9 center sc on next end, 2 sc in next st, (sc in next st, 2 sc in next st) 4 times; repeat from *, sc around, join with sl st in first sc (424 sc).

Rnd 6: Ch 3, dc in next st, dc in next st and in tip of corresponding spike at same time, (dc in each of next 2 sts, dc in next st and in tip of next spike at same time) 64 times, *(dc in each of next 2 sts, 2 dc in next st) 2 times, dc in each of next 2 sts*, dc in next st and in tip of next spike at same time; repeat between **, (dc in each of next 2 sts, dc in next st and in tip of next spike at same time) 65 times; repeat between **, dc in next st and in tip of next spike at same time; repeat between **, join with sl st in top of ch-3, fasten off.

Hold Strips wrong sides together, matching sts; working in **back lps** *(see fig. 1, pg. 158)*, sew Strips together leaving 21 sts on each end unsewn.

Tassel (make 24)
For each Tassel, cut 22 strands each 14" long. Tie separate strand tightly around middle of all strands; fold strands in half. Wrap 20" strand 1" from top of fold, covering ½"; secure. Trim ends.

Tie Tassels to ends of Strips.✤

Fantasy Shells

elizabeth a. white, designer

Escape for an interlude of refreshing relaxation. Shimmering shells create delightful allure in this light and airy throw with a Victorian look.

Finished Size
46" x 66" without fringe

Materials
Worsted-weight yarn — 36 oz. rose; I crochet hook or size needed to obtain gauge.

Gauge
1 shell = 1½"; 1 shell row and 1 V-st row = 2¼".

Skill Level
★ Easy

Instructions

Afghan

Notes: For **V-st,** (tr, ch 1, tr) in next st.

For **shell,** 5 tr in next st.

Row 1: Ch 137, shell in 5th ch from hook, (skip next 3 chs, V-st in next ch, skip next 3 chs, shell in next ch) across to last 4 chs, skip next 3 chs, tr in last ch, turn (17 shells, 16 V-sts, 2 tr).

Row 2: Ch 4, V-st in 3rd st of next shell, (shell in ch sp of next V-st, V-st in 3rd st of next shell) across, tr in last st, turn.

Row 3: Ch 4, shell in next V-st, (V-st in 3rd st of next shell, shell in next V-st) across, tr in last st, turn.

Rows 4-59: Repeat rows 2 and 3 alternately. At end of last row, fasten off.

Fringe

For **each Fringe,** cut six strands each 20" long. With all strands held together, fold in half, insert hook in st or sp, draw fold through st or sp, draw all loose ends through fold, tighten. Trim ends.

Fringe in first and last st and in sp between each V-st and shell on short ends of afghan.✤

Starglow

denise cheek, designer

Dazzle friends and family with bursts of brilliant color on an onyx background. Super-easy motifs are sewn together for fast assembly.

Finished Size
48" x 68"

Materials
Worsted-weight yarn — 22 oz. black, 3½ oz. dk. aqua, 2½ oz. each dk. pink, dk. coral, lt. aqua, lt. gray and dk. gray, 2 oz. each lt. coral, dk. purple and lt. pink, 1½ oz. lt. purple; tapestry needle; I crochet hook or size needed to obtain gauge.

Gauge
Rnd 1 of Large Motif = 2½" across;
Large Motif is 10" across from point to point.
Small Motif is 4¼" across.

Skill Level
★ Easy

Instructions

Large Motif (make 12 lt. green/dk. green, 9 lt. pink/dk. pink, 8 lt. coral/dk. coral, 6 lt. purple/dk. purple)

Rnd 1: With lt. color, ch 5, sl st in first ch to form ring, ch 3, 23 dc in ring, join with sl st in top of ch-3 (24 dc).

Rnd 2: Ch 1, sc in first st, ch 9, skip next 2 sts, (sc in next st, ch 9, skip next 2 sts) around, join with sl st in first sc, fasten off (8 ch lps).

Rnd 3: Join dk. color with sl st in any ch lp, ch 3, (3 dc, ch 2, 4 dc) in same lp, (4 dc, ch 2, 4 dc) in each ch lp around, join with sl st in top of ch-3, fasten off (64 dc, 8 ch-2 sps).

Rnd 4: Join black with sc in any ch-2 sp, ch 7, (sc in next ch sp, ch 7) around, join with sl st in first sc (8 sc, 8 ch lps).

Rnd 5: Ch 1, (sc, ch 2, sc) in first st, 7 sc in next ch lp, *(sc, ch 2, sc) in next st, 7 sc in next ch lp; repeat from * around, join (72 sc, 8 ch-2 sps).

Rnd 6: Ch 3, dc in each st around with 4 dc in each ch-2 sp, join with sl st in top of ch-3, fasten off (104 dc).

Small Motif (make 24)

Rnd 1: With lt. gray, ch 5, sl st in first ch to form ring, ch 3, 2 dc in ring, ch 5, (3 dc in ring, ch 5) 3 times, join with sl st in top of ch-3, fasten off (12 dc, 4 ch-5 sps).

Rnd 2: Join dk. gray with sl st in any ch sp, ch 3, (2 dc, ch 2, 3 dc) in same sp, ch 2; *for **corner,** (3 dc, ch 2, 3 dc) in next ch sp; ch 2; repeat from * around, join, fasten off (24 dc, 8 ch-2 sps).

Rnd 3: Join black with sc in any corner ch sp, 3 sc in same sp, (*sc in each of next 3 sts, 3 sc in next ch sp, sc in each of next 3 sts*, 4 sc in next corner ch sp) 3 times; repeat between **, join with sl st in first sc, fasten off.

With tapestry needle and black, sew points of Large and Small Motifs together according to Assembly Diagram.✤

ASSEMBLY DIAGRAM

Small Motif

Large Motif
A = Lt. aqua /dk. aqua
B = Lt. pink /dk. pink
C = Lt. coral /dk. coral
D = Lt. purple /dk. purple

A	C	A	C	A
B	D	B	D	B
A	C	A	C	A
B	D	B	D	B
A	C	A	C	A
B	D	B	D	B
A	C	A	C	A

Patchwork Quilts

As enduring as the time-honored art they portray, quilt-style afghans evoke visions of an era when no well-dressed home was without a cornucopia of needlework. Crochet your own re-creations of these striking designs to bring warmth and ambiance to your home.

Berry Patch

nancy e. quail, designer

Deliciously ripe hues of fruity pinks lend mouth-watering sweetness to this quaint coverlet. Topped with a generous dollop of fringe, it's purely delectable.

Finished Size
45" x 58"

Materials
Worsted-weight yarn — 20 oz. each med. rose and dk. rose, 16½ oz. lt. rose; H crochet hook or size needed to obtain gauge.

Gauge
7 dc sts = 2"; 2 dc rows = 1".

Skill Level
★ Easy

Instructions
First Motif

Rnd 1: With med. rose, ch 6, sl st in first ch to form ring, ch 4, (dc in ring, ch 1) 11 times, join with sl st in 3rd ch of ch-4 (12 dc, 12 ch sps).

Rnd 2: Ch 3, 2 dc in next ch sp, dc in next st, ch 2, skip next ch sp, (dc in next st, 2 dc in next ch sp, dc in next st, ch 2, skip next ch sp) around, join with sl st in top of ch-3 (24 dc, 6 ch sps).

Rnd 3: Ch 3, dc in same st, (*dc in each of next 2 sts, 2 dc in next st, ch 2, skip next ch sp*, 2 dc in next st) 5 times; repeat between **, join (36 dc, 6 ch sps).

Rnd 4: Ch 3, dc in same st, (*dc in next 4 sts, 2 dc in next st, ch 2, skip next ch sp*, 2 dc in next st) 5 times; repeat between **, join (48 dc, 6 ch sps).

Rnd 5: Ch 3, dc in next 7 sts, ch 3, sc in next ch sp, ch 3, (dc in next 8 sts, ch 3, sc in next ch sp, ch 3) around, join (48 dc, 12 ch sps, 6 sc).

Rnd 6: Sl st in next st, ch 3, dc in next 5 sts, (ch 3, skip next st, sc in next ch sp) 2 times, ch 3, skip next st, *dc in next 6 sts, (ch 3, skip next st, sc in next ch sp) 2 times, ch 3, skip next st; repeat from * around, join (36 dc, 18 ch sps, 12 sc).

Rnd 7: Sl st in next st, ch 3, dc in each of next 3 sts, (ch 3, skip next st, sc in next ch sp) 3 times, ch 3, skip next st, *dc in next 4 sts, (ch 3, skip next st, sc in next ch sp) 3 times, ch 3, skip next st; repeat from * around, join (24 dc, 24 ch sps, 18 sc).

Rnd 8: Sl st in next st, ch 3, dc in next st, (ch 3, skip next st, sc in next ch sp) 4 times, ch 3, skip next st, *dc in each of next 2 sts, (ch 3, skip next st, sc in next ch sp) 4 times, ch 3, skip next st; repeat from * around, join (30 ch sps, 24 sc, 12 dc).

Rnd 9: Sl st in next st, (sl st, ch 3, 2 dc) in next ch sp, (ch 1, 3 dc in next ch sp) 4 times, ch 3, *(3 dc in next ch sp, ch 1) 4 times, 3 dc in next ch sp, ch 3; repeat from * around, join, fasten off.

Second Motif

Rnds 1-8: With dk. rose (see Joining Diagram on pg. 43), repeat same rnds of First Motif.

Rnd 9: Sl st in next st, (sl st, ch 3, 2 dc) in next ch sp, (ch 1, 3 dc in next ch sp) 4 times; to **join,** holding Motifs wrong sides tog, ch 1, sl st in corresponding ch-3 sp on other Motif, ch 1, 3 dc in next ch sp on this Motif, (sl st in next corresponding ch-1 sp on other Motif, 3 dc in next ch sp on this Motif) 4 times, ch 1, sl st in next corresponding ch-3 sp on other

Continued on page 43

Evening Stars

katherine eng, designer

Twinkle, twinkle little star — how very beautiful you are! Twilight shades of celestial blue and green create a heavenly throw adorned with jeweltone stars.

Finished Size
39" x 59"

Materials
Worsted-weight yarn — 15½ oz. each green and blue, 11½ oz. each aqua and rose; tapestry needle; G crochet hook or size needed to obtain gauge.

Gauge
4 sc sts = 1"; 4 sc rows = 1".
Each Square is 10" x 10".

Skill Level
★★ Average

Instructions

Square No. 1 (make 8)

Rnd 1: With rose, ch 4, sl st in first ch to form ring, ch 1, 8 sc in ring, join with sl st in first sc (8 sc).

Rnd 2: Ch 1, 2 sc in each st around, join, fasten off (16).

Rnd 3: Join green with sc in any st, ch 2, sc in same st, skip next st, *(sc, ch 2, sc) in next st, skip next st; repeat from * around, join, fasten off (16 sc, 8 ch-2 sps).

Note: For **shell,** (2 dc, ch 2, 2 dc) in next ch sp.

Rnd 4: Join rose with sl st in any ch-2 sp, ch 3, (dc, ch 2, 2 dc) in same sp, shell in each ch-2 sp around, join with sl st in top of ch-3 (8 shells).

Rnd 5: Ch 1, *[sc in next dc, (sc, ch 3, sc) in next ch sp, sc in next dc], sl st in each of next 2 dc; repeat from * 6 more times; repeat between [ ], sl st in next st, sl st in joining sl st of last rnd, join with sl st in first sc.

Rnd 6: Ch 1, sc in first st, *[hdc in next st, (2 dc, ch 3, 2 dc) in next ch sp, hdc in next st, sc in next st, ch 1, skip next 2 sl sts], sc in next sc; repeat from * 6 more times; repeat between [ ], join, fasten off.

Rnd 7: Join green with sc in any st; skipping ch-1 sps, sc in each st around with (sc, ch 3, sc) in each ch-3 sp, join, fasten off.

Rnd 8: Join rose with sc in 2nd st after any ch-3 sp, *[sc in each of next 2 sts, ch 1, skip next 2 sts, sc in each of next 3 sts, hdc in next st, (2 dc, ch 3, 2 dc) in next ch sp, hdc in next st], sc in next st; repeat from * 6 more times; repeat between [ ], join.

Rnd 9: Ch 1, sc in each st and sl st in each ch-1 sp around with (2 sc, ch 3, 2 sc) in each ch-3 sp, join, fasten off.

Rnd 10: Join aqua with sl st in any ch-3 sp, *ch 1, sc in next 7 sts, skip next sc, next sl st and next sc, (sl st in each of next 2 sts on rnd 9, **turn,** ch 1, sc in next 7 sts, **turn,** ch 1, sc in next 7 sts) 3 times, sl st in next st on rnd 9, sl st in next ch-3 sp, **turn,** sc in next 7 sts, **turn,** ch 1, sc in next 7 sts, sl st in same ch-3 sp on rnd 9, sc in each of next 2 sts, hdc in each of next 2 sts, dc in each of next 2 sts, tr in next st, yo 2 times, insert hook in next sc, yo, draw lp through, skip next sl st, insert hook in next sc, yo, draw lp through, (yo, draw through 2 lps on hook) 4 times, tr in next st, dc in each of next 2 sts, hdc in each of next 2 sts, sc in each of next 2 sts, sl st in next ch-3 sp; repeat from * 3 more times, fasten off.

Rnd 11: Join aqua with sc in any corner, ch 2, sc in same corner, *evenly space 31 sc

Continued on page 42

Evening Stars

Continued from page 41

across to next corner, (sc, ch 2, sc) in next corner; repeat from * 2 more times, evenly space 31 sc across, join, fasten off.

Rnd 12: Join green with sc in any corner ch sp, ch 2, sc in same sp, *[ch 1, skip next st, (sc in next st, ch 1, skip next st) across to next corner], (sc, ch 2, sc) in next corner ch sp; repeat from * 2 more times; repeat between [ ], join, **turn.**

Rnd 13: Sl st in next ch sp, ch 1, sc in same sp, *ch 1, (sc in next ch sp, ch 1) across to next corner ch sp, (sc, ch 3, sc) in next corner ch sp; repeat from * 3 more times, ch 1, join, **turn.**

Rnd 14: Ch 1, sc in each st and in each ch-1 sp around with (sc, ch 3, sc) in each corner ch-3 sp, join, fasten off (39 sts on each side, 4 ch sps).

Square No. 2 (make 7)

Substituting blue for rose, work same as Square No. 1.

Holding Squares wrong sides together, with green, sew together through **back lps** *(see fig. 1, pg. 158)* according to Assembly Diagram.

Border

Rnd 1: Join green with sc in corner ch sp on one short end, ch 2, sc in same sp, sc in each st, hdc in each ch-3 sp on each side of seams and hdc in each seam around with (sc, ch 3, sc) in each corner ch sp, join with sl st in first sc (125 sts on each short end, 209 sts on each long edge).

Rnd 2: Sl st in next corner ch sp, ch 1, (sc, ch 3, sc) in same sp, *[ch 1, skip next st, (sc in next st, ch 1, skip next st) across to next corner], (sc, ch 3, sc) in next corner ch sp; repeat from * 2 more times; repeat between [ ], join, **turn.**

Rnds 3-4: Repeat rnds 13-14 of Square No. 1. At end of last rnd, **turn.**

Rnd 5: Join blue with sc in any ch-3 sp, ch 3, sc in same sp, *[ch 2, skip next 2 sts, (sc in next st, ch 2, skip next 2 sts) across to next corner], (sc, ch 3, sc) in next corner ch sp; repeat from * 2 more times; repeat between [ ], join, **turn.**

Rnd 6: Ch 3, 2 dc in each ch-2 sp and dc in each sc around with (2 dc, ch 3, 2 dc) in each

ASSEMBLY DIAGRAM

Square No. 1	Square No. 2	Square No. 1
Square No. 2	Square No. 1	Square No. 2
Square No. 1	Square No. 2	Square No. 1
Square No. 2	Square No. 1	Square No. 2
Square No. 1	Square No. 2	Square No. 1

corner ch sp, join with sl st in top of ch-3, **do not** turn.

Rnd 7: Ch 1, sc in first st, skip next 2 sts, *[(shell in next st, skip next 2 sts, sc in next st, skip next 2 sts) across to next corner ch sp, (3 dc, ch 3, 3 dc) in next corner ch sp, skip next 2 sts], sc in next st; repeat from * 2 more times; repeat between [ ], join with sl st in first sc, **turn.**

Rnd 8: Ch 3, (dc, ch 2, 2 dc) in same st, skip next dc, sc in next dc, *[(3 dc, ch 3, 3 dc) in next corner ch sp, skip next dc, sc in next dc, skip next dc], shell in next sc, (sc in ch sp of next shell, shell in next sc) across to next corner, skip next dc, sc in next dc, skip next dc; repeat from * 2 more times; repeat between [ ], (shell in next sc, sc in ch sp of next shell) across, join with sl st in top of ch-3, **turn.**

Rnd 9: Sl st in next sc, ch 3, shell in each shell and dc in each sc around with (3 dc, ch 3, 3 dc) in each corner ch sp, join, **turn.**

Rnd 10: Ch 3, (dc, ch 2, 2 dc) in same st, sc in next shell, shell in next dc, skip next dc, sc in next dc, *[(3 dc, ch 3, 3 dc) in next corner ch sp, skip next dc, sc in next dc, skip next dc], shell in next dc, (sc in next shell, shell in next dc) across to next corner, skip next dc, sc in next dc, skip next dc; repeat from * 2 more times; repeat between [ ], (shell in next dc, sc in next shell) across, join, **turn,** fasten off.

Rnd 11: Join green with sl st in first sc after any corner, ch 3, (dc, ch 2, 2 dc) in same st, *[(sc in next shell, shell in next sc) across to next corner, skip next dc, sc in next dc, skip next dc, (3 dc, ch 3, 3 dc) in next corner ch sp, skip next dc, sc in next dc, skip next dc], shell in next sc; repeat from * 2 more times; repeat between [ ], join, **do not** turn, fasten off.

Rnd 12: Join rose with sl st in first sc after any corner, *[ch 3, (sl st, ch 3, sl st) in next shell, ch 3, sl st in next sc; repeat from * across to next corner, ch 2, skip next dc, sl st in next dc, ch 2, skip next dc, (sl st, ch 3, sl st, ch 5, sl st, ch 3, sl st) in next corner ch sp, ch 2, skip next dc, sl st in next dc, ch 2, skip next dc], sl st in next sc; repeat from * 2 more times; repeat between [ ], join with sl st in first sl st, fasten off.✤

Berry Patch

Continued from page 38

Motif, ch 1, *3 dc in next ch sp on this Motif, (ch 1, 3 dc in next ch sp) 4 times, ch 3; repeat from * 3 more times, join, fasten off.

Using colors shown in diagram, repeat Second Motif 3 more times.

Remaining Motifs

Using colors shown in diagram, work same as Second Motif, joining on one or two sides as needed.

Half Motif (make 3 med. rose, 3 dk. rose as shown in diagram)

Row 1: Ch 6, sl st in first ch to form ring, ch 4, dc in ring, (ch 1, dc in ring) 4 times, turn (6 dc, 5 ch sps).

Row 2: Ch 3, dc in same st, ch 2, skip next ch sp, (dc in next st, 2 dc in next ch sp, dc in next st, ch 2, skip next ch sp) 2 times, 2 dc in last st, turn (12 dc, 3 ch sps).

Row 3: Ch 3, 2 dc in next st, ch 2, skip next ch sp, (2 dc in next st, dc in each of next 2 sts, 2 dc in next st, ch 2, skip next ch sp) 2 times, 2 dc in next st, dc in last st, turn (18 dc, 3 ch sps).

Row 4: Ch 3, dc in next st, 2 dc in next st, ch 2, skip next ch sp, (2 dc in next st, dc in next 4 sts, 2 dc in next st, ch 2, skip next ch sp) 2 times, 2 dc in next st, dc in each of last 2 sts, turn (24 dc, 3 ch sps).

Row 5: Ch 3, dc in each of next 3 sts, ch 3, sc in next ch sp, ch 3, (dc in next 8 sts, ch 3, sc in next ch sp, ch 3) 2 times, dc in last 4 sts, turn (24 dc, 6 ch sps, 3 sc).

Row 6: Ch 3, dc in each of next 2 sts, *(ch 3, skip next st, sc in next ch sp) 2 times, ch 3, skip next st, dc in next 6 sts; repeat from *, (ch 3, skip next st, sc in next ch sp) 2 times, ch 2, skip next st, dc in each of last 3 sts, turn (18 dc, 9 ch sps, 6 sc).

Row 7: Ch 3, dc in next st, *(ch 3, skip next st, sc in next ch sp) 3 times, ch 3, skip next st, dc in next 4 sts; repeat from *, (ch 3, skip next st, sc in next ch sp) 3 times, ch 3, skip next st, dc in each of last 2 sts, turn (12 dc, 12 ch sps, 9 sc).

Row 8: Ch 6, *(sc in next ch sp, ch 3) 4 times, skip next st, dc in each of next 2 sts, ch 3; repeat from *, (sc in next ch sp, ch 3) 4 times, dc in last st, turn.

Row 9: Ch 3, sl st in corresponding ch-3 sp on other Motif — see Joining Diagram, 3 dc in next ch sp on this Motif, *(sl st in next ch-1 sp on other Motif, 3 dc in next ch sp on this Motif) 4 times, ch 1, sl st in next ch-3 sp on other Motif, ch 1, 3 dc in next ch sp on this Motif; repeat from *; repeat between ( ) 4 times, sl st in next ch-3 sp on other Motif, dc in 3rd ch of ch-6, fasten off.

Edging

Working around entire outer edge, evenly spacing sts so edge lays flat, join with sc in any st, sc around, join with sl st in first sc, fasten off.

Fringe

For **each Fringe,** cut two strands of each color each 12" long. With all six strands held together, fold in half, insert hook in st, draw fold through st, draw all loose ends through fold, tighten. Trim ends.

Fringe in every other st on each short end of afghan.✸

JOINING DIAGRAM

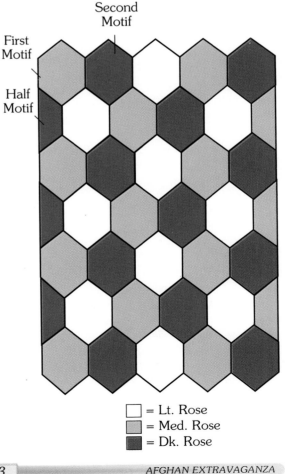

☐ = Lt. Rose
▨ = Med. Rose
■ = Dk. Rose

Woven Velvet

elizabeth a. white, designer

Soft as petals floating on a balmy breeze, this light and airy afghan is the perfect year-round companion. Subtle colors and a gentle woven texture evoke a captivating effect.

Finished Size
48" x 60" without fringe

Materials
Fuzzy bulky-weight yarn — 23 oz. each off-white and green, 19 oz. rose; I crochet hook or size needed to obtain gauge.

Gauge
3 dc sts and 2 ch-1 sps = 1½";
7 dc rows = 4".

Skill Level
★ Easy

Instructions
Afghan
Row 1: With off-white, ch 162, dc in 6th ch from hook, (ch 1, skip next ch, dc in next ch) across, turn (80 dc).

Row 2: Ch 4, dc in next dc, (ch 1, dc in next dc) across to ch-5, ch 1, skip next ch, dc in next ch, turn. Ch-4 counts as one dc and one ch-1 sp.

Row 3: Ch 4, dc in next dc, (ch 1, dc in next dc) across, turn.

Rows 4-9: Repeat row 3. At end of last row, fasten off.

Row 10: Join green with sl st in first st, ch 4, dc in next dc, (ch 1, dc in next dc) across, turn.

Rows 11-16: Repeat row 3. At end of last row, fasten off.

Row 17: With rose, repeat row 10.

Rows 18-25: Repeat row 3. At end of last row, fasten off.

Rows 26-32: Repeat rows 10-16.

Row 33: With off-white, repeat row 10.

Rows 34-41: Repeat row 3. At end of last row, fasten off.

Row 42: With rose, repeat row 10.

Rows 43-48: Repeat row 3. At end of last row, fasten off.

Row 49: Repeat row 10.

Rows 50-57: Repeat row 3. At end of last row, fasten off.

Row 58: With rose, repeat row 10.

Rows 59-64: Repeat row 3. At end of last row, fasten off.

Row 65: With off-white, repeat row 10.

Rows 66-73: Repeat row 3. At end of last row, fasten off.

Rows 74-80: Repeat rows 10-16.

Row 81: With rose, repeat row 10.

Rows 82-89: Repeat row 3. At end of last row, fasten off.

Rows 90-96: Repeat rows 10-16.

Row 97: With off-white, repeat row 10.

Rows 98-105: Repeat row 3. At end of last row, fasten off.

Finishing
Cut 84 strands off-white, 81 strands green, and 72 strands rose each 84" long.

Leaving 12" ends for fringe, holding 3 strands together, weave through ch-1 sps from top to bottom (alternate weaving pattern from front to back on every other row), working across width of afghan as follows: seven rows off-white, five rows green, seven rows rose, five rows green, seven rows off-white, five rows rose, seven rows green, five rows rose, seven rows off-white, five rows green, seven rows rose, five rows green and seven rows off-white. ❧

Autumn Lights

katherine eng, designer

The dusky glow of a dewy fall evening will linger in your thoughts as you gaze upon the mingled shades of purple, lilac and green in this mesmerizing quilt-look afghan.

Finished Size
44¾" x 60¼"

Materials
Worsted-weight yarn — 22 oz. navy, 18½ oz. purple, 11 oz. each green and lilac; G crochet hook or size needed to obtain gauge.

Gauge
4 sc sts = 1"; 4 sc rows = 1". Each Block is 7¾" square.

Skill Level
★★ Average

Instructions
Block (make 35)
Section No. 1
Row 1: With lilac, ch 15, sc in 2nd ch from hook, sc in each ch across, turn (14 sc).

Rows 2-5: Ch 1, 2 sc in first st, sc in each st across with 2 sc in last st, turn. At end of last row, **do not** turn (22), fasten off.

Section No. 2
Row 1: Join navy with sc in end of row 1 on Section No. 1 (see Block Diagram on pg. 48), sc in end of each row across, turn (5 sc).

Rows 2-10: Ch 1, 2 sc in first st, sc in each st across with 2 sc in last st, turn. At end of last row (23), fasten off.

Section No. 3
Row 1: Working in starting ch on opposite side of row 1 on Section No. 1, join green with sc in first ch, sc next 2 chs tog, sc in each ch across, sl st in end of row 1 on Section No. 2, sl st in next row, turn (13 sc).

Row 2: Ch 1, sc in each sc across to last 2 sts, sc last 2 sts tog, turn (12).

Row 3: Ch 1, sc first 2 sts tog, sc in each st across, sl st in next row on Section No. 2, turn (11).

Row 4: Repeat row 2 (10).

Row 5: Repeat row 3 with sl st in each of next 2 rows on Section No. 2 (9).

Rows 6-7: Repeat rows 2 and 5 (8, 7).

Rows 8-12: Repeat rows 2 and 3 alternately, ending with row 2 and 2 sts.

Row 13: Ch 1, sc next 2 sts tog, sl st in end of last row on Section No. 2, turn (1).

Row 14: Ch 1, sc in next sc, turn, fasten off.

Section No. 4
Row 1: Join green with sc in end of last row on Section No. 2, evenly space 13 more sc across ends of rows, sc in next 8 sts on Section No. 1, turn (22 sc).

Rows 2-5: Ch 1, sc first 2 sts tog, sc in each st across to last 2 sts, sc last 2 sts tog, turn. At end of last row, **do not** turn (14), fasten off.

Section No. 5
Row 1: Join navy with sc in end of last row on Section No. 4, sc in end of each row across, sl st in each of next 2 sts on Section No. 1, turn (5 sc).

Row 2: Ch 1, 2 sc in first sc, sc in each sc across with 2 sc in last sc, turn (7).

Row 3: Repeat row 2, skip next st on Section No. 1, sl st in each of next 2 sts on Section No. 1, turn (9).

Rows 4-10: Repeat rows 2 and 3 alternately, ending with row 2. At end of last

Continued on page 48

Autumn Lights

Continued from page 47
row (23), fasten off.

Section No. 6

Row 1: Join lilac with sc in first st of last row on Section No. 4, sc next 2 sts tog, sc in each st across, sl st in end of row 1 on Section No. 5, sl st in next row, turn (13 sc).

Row 2: Ch 1, sc in each sc across to last 2 sts, sc last 2 sts tog, turn (12).

Row 3: Ch 1, sc first 2 sts tog, sc in each st across, sl st in end of next row on Section No. 5, turn (11).

Row 4: Repeat row 2 (10).

Row 5: Repeat row 3 with sl st in end of each of next 2 rows on Section No. 5 (9).

Rows 6-7: Repeat rows 2 and 5 (8, 7).

Rows 8-12: Repeat rows 2 and 3 alternately, ending with row 2 and 2 sts.

Row 13: Ch 1, sc next 2 sts tog, sl st in last row on Section No. 5, turn (1).

Row 14: Ch 1, sc in next st, turn, fasten off.

Edging

Rnd 1: Join purple with sc in any corner, ch 2, sc in same corner, *evenly space 25 sc across to next corner, (sc, ch 2, sc) in next corner; repeat from * 2 more times, evenly space 25 sc across, join with sl st in first sc (108 sc).

Rnd 2: Ch 1, sc in each st around with (sc, ch 2, sc) in each corner ch sp, join, fasten off.

Working in **front lps** only *(see fig. 1, pg. 158)*, with purple, sew Blocks together according to Assembly Diagram.

Border

Rnd 1: Join purple with sc in corner ch sp on one short end, ch 3, sc in same sp, sc in each st, hdc in each ch-2 sp on each side of seams and hdc in each seam around with (sc, ch 3, sc) in each corner ch sp, join with sl st in first sc, **turn** (159 sts on each short end, 223 sts on each long edge).

Rnd 2: Sl st in next st, ch 1, sc in same st, ch 1, skip next st, (sc in next st, ch 1, skip next st) across to next corner ch sp, *(sc, ch 3, sc) in next corner ch sp, ch 1, skip next st, (sc in next st, ch 1, skip next st) across to next corner ch sp; repeat from * 2 more times, (sc, ch 3, sc) in next corner ch sp, ch 1, skip next st, join, **turn.**

Rnd 3: Ch 1, sc in each st and in each ch-1 sp around with (sc, ch 3, sc) in each corner ch

sp, join, **do not** turn, fasten off.

Rnd 4: Join navy with sc in 2nd st after corner ch sp on short end, *[skip next st, (3 dc in next st, skip next st, sc in next st, skip next st) across to next corner ch sp, 5 dc in next corner ch sp, skip next st], sc in next st; repeat from * 2 more times; repeat between [ ], join, **turn.**

Rnd 5: Ch 3, 2 dc in same st, *[sc in 2nd dc of next corner 5-dc group, 5 dc in next dc, sc in next dc, skip next dc], 3 dc in next sc, (sc in center dc of next 3-dc group, 3 dc in next sc) across to next corner; repeat from * 2 more times; repeat between [ ], (3 dc in next sc, sc in center st of next 3-dc group) across, join with sl st in top of ch-3, **turn.**

Rnd 6: Sl st in next sc, ch 3, 2 dc in same st, *(sc in center st of next 3-dc group, 3 dc in next sc) across to next corner, sc in 2nd dc of next corner 5-dc group, 5 dc in next dc, sc in next dc, skip next dc, 3 dc in next sc; repeat from * 3 more times, sc in center st of next 3-dc group, join, **turn.**

Rnd 7: Sl st to center st of next 3-dc group, ch 1, sc in same st, ch 3, *[sc in first st of next corner 5-dc group, ch 3, skip next dc, (sc, ch 3, sc) in next dc, ch 3, skip next dc, sc in next dc, ch 3, (sc in center of next 3-dc group, ch 3) across] to next corner 5-dc group; repeat from * 2 more times; repeat between [ ], join

BLOCK DIAGRAM

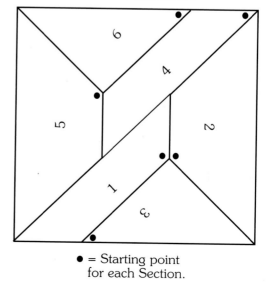

● = Starting point
for each Section.

with sl st in first sc, **turn.**

Note: For **shell,** (3 dc, ch 3, 3 dc) in next ch sp.

Rnd 8: Sl st in next ch sp, ch 1, sc in same sp, ch 1, shell in next ch sp, ch 1, (sc in next ch sp, ch 1, shell in next ch sp, ch 1) around, join, **do not** turn, fasten off.

Rnd 9: Join purple with sl st in ch sp of any shell, ch 2, sl st in same ch sp, ch 2, skip next dc, sl st in next dc, ch 2, skip next dc, sl st in next sc, ch 2, skip next dc, sl st in next dc, ch 2, *(sl st, ch 2, sl st) in next ch sp, ch 2, skip next dc, sl st in next dc, ch 2, skip next dc, sl st in next sc, ch 2, skip next dc, sl st in next dc, ch 2; repeat from * around, join, fasten off.✣

ASSEMBLY DIAGRAM

Baby Card Tricks

katherine eng, designer

Pinwheels of rose and lavender on a lavish aqua background add lighthearted luster to this precious baby cover that's just the right size for baby's first excursions.

Finished Size
32" x 38½"

Materials
Worsted-weight yarn — 19 oz. aqua, 5 oz. each lavender and rose; safety or bobby pin for marker; tapestry needle; G crochet hook or size needed to obtain gauge.

Gauge
2 sc sts and 2 ch-1 sps = 1"; 4 sc rows = 1". Each Block is 6½" square.

Skill Level
★★ Average

Instructions

Block (make 35)

Section No. 1

Row 1: With lavender, ch 6, sc in 2nd ch from hook, (ch 1, skip next ch, sc in next ch) across, turn (3 sc, 2 ch-1 sps). Mark center st of row 1 for front of Block. Leave marker in until Block is completed.

Rows 2-5: Ch 1, sc in first st, (ch 1, skip next ch-1 sp, sc in next st) across, turn. At end of last row, **do not** turn, fasten off.

Section No. 2

Row 1: Join rose with sl st in ch at base of first st on row 1 of Section No. 1 (see Block Diagram on pg. 53), ch 6, sc in 2nd ch from hook, (ch 1, skip next ch, sc in next ch) across, sl st in end of row 1 on Section No. 1, turn (3 sc, 2 ch-1 sps).

Row 2: Ch 1, sc in first st, (ch 1, skip next ch-1 sp, sc in next st) across, turn.

Row 3: Ch 1, sc in first st, (ch 1, skip next ch-1 sp, sc in next st) across, sl st in end of row 3 on Section No. 1, turn.

Row 4: Repeat row 2.

Row 5: Ch 1, sc in first st, (ch 1, skip next ch-1 sp, sc in next st) across, sl st in first st of row 5 on Section No. 1, **do not** turn, fasten off.

Section No. 3

Row 1: Working in starting ch on opposite side of row 1 on Section No. 2, join lavender with sc in first ch, (ch 1, skip next ch, sc in next ch) across, turn (3 sc, 2 ch-1 sps).

Rows 2-5: Repeat rows 2-5 of Section No. 1.

Section No. 4

Row 1: Working in starting ch on opposite side of row 1 on Section No. 1, join rose with sc in first ch, (ch 1, skip next ch, sc in next ch) across, sl st in end of row 1 on Section No. 3, turn (3 sc, 2 ch-1 sps).

Rows 2-5: Working sl sts in end of rows on Section No. 3, repeat rows 2-5 of Section No. 2.

Section No. 5

Row 1: Join rose with sc in first st of row 5 on Section No. 2, (ch 1, skip next ch-1 sp, sc in next st) 2 times, ch 1, sc in first st on next Section; repeat between ( ) 2 times, turn (6 sc, 5 ch-1 sps).

Rows 2-5: Repeat rows 2-5 of Section No. 1.

Section No. 6

Joining in first st of Section No. 4, work same as Section No. 5.

Section No. 7

Row 1: Working in ends of rows on

Continued on page 52

Baby Card Tricks

Continued from page 50

Section No. 3, join lavender with sc in end of row 5, (ch 1, skip next row, sc in end of next row) 2 times, ch 1, sc in end of row 1 on next Section; repeat between ( ) 2 times, turn (6 sc, 5 ch-1 sps).

Rows 2-5: Repeat rows 2-5 of Section No. 1.

Section No. 8

Joining in end of row 5 on Section No. 1, work same as Section No. 7.

Section No. 9

Row 1: Join aqua with sc in end of row 5 on Section No. 5, sc in end of next 4 rows, sl st in end of row 1 on next Section, turn (5 sc).

Row 2: Ch 1, sc in each st across to last 2 sts, sc last 2 sts tog, turn (4).

Row 3: Ch 1, sc first 2 sts tog, sc in each st across, sl st in end of row 3 on next Section, turn (3 sc).

Row 4: Ch 1, sc in first st, sc last 2 sts tog, turn (2).

Row 5: Ch 1, sc next 2 sts tog, sl st in first st on row 5 of next Section, fasten off.

Repeat on Sections No. 6-8.

Section No. 10

Row 1: Join aqua with sc in first st of row 5 on Section No. 5, sc in each ch sp and in each st across, turn (11 sc).

Rows 2-5: Ch 1, sc first 2 sts tog, sc in each st across to last 2 sts, sc last 2 sts tog, turn, ending with 3 sts in last row.

Row 6: Ch 1, sc first and 2nd sts tog, ch 2, sc 2nd and 3rd sts tog, turn, fasten off.

Repeat on Sections No. 6-8.

Edging

With right side facing you, working around outer edge, join aqua with sc in any corner ch-2 sp, ch 3, sc in same sp, *evenly space 25 sc across to next corner, (sc, ch 3, sc) in next corner ch-2 sp; repeat from * 2 more times, evenly space 25 sc across, join with sl st in first sc, fasten off (108 sc).

Working in **back lps** *(see fig. 1, pg. 158)*, with aqua, sew Blocks together according to Assembly Diagram.

Border

Rnd 1: Join aqua with sc in corner ch sp on one short end, ch 3, sc in same sp, sc in each st, hdc in each ch-3 sp on each side of seams and hdc in each seam around with (sc, ch 3, sc) in each corner ch sp, join with sl st in first sc, **turn** (119 sts on each short end, 149 sts on each long edge).

Rnd 2: Sl st in next st, ch 1, sc in same st, *ch 1, skip next st, (sc in next st, ch 1, skip next st) across to next corner ch sp, (sc, ch 3, sc) in next corner ch sp; repeat from * 3 more times, ch 1, skip last st, join, **turn.**

Rnd 3: Ch 1, sc in each st and in each ch-1 sp around with (sc, ch 3, sc) in each corner ch sp, join, **do not** turn.

Rnd 4: Sl st in each of next 2 sts, ch 1, sc in same st as last sl st, ch 1, skip next st, *[(sc, ch 3, sc) in next corner ch sp, ch 2, skip next st], sc in next st, (ch 2, skip next 2 sts, sc in next st) across to one st before next corner ch sp, ch 2, skip next st; repeat from * 2 more times; repeat between [ ], (sc in next st, ch 2, skip next 2 sts) across, join.

Rnd 5: Sl st in next ch-2 sp, ch 1, (sc, ch 2, sc) in same sp, (sc, ch 2, sc) in each ch-2 sp around with (sc, ch 3, sc) in each corner ch sp, join.

Rnd 6: Sl st in next ch-2 sp, ch 1, (sc, ch 2, sc) in same sp, (sc, ch 2, sc) in each ch-2 sp around with (sc, ch 2, sc, ch 3, sc, ch 2, sc) in each corner ch-3 sp, join, **turn.**

Rnd 7: Sl st in next ch-2 sp, ch 1, sc in same sp, ch 2, (sc in next ch-2 sp, ch 2) around with (sc, ch 3, sc, ch 2) in each corner ch-3 sp, join, **turn,** fasten off.

Note: For **shell,** (2 dc, ch 2, 2 dc) in next ch sp.

Rnd 8: Join lavender with sc in first ch-2 sp after any corner ch-3 sp, *[(shell in next ch sp, sc in next ch sp) across to next corner ch-3 sp, (3 dc, ch 3, 3 dc) in next corner ch sp], sc in next ch sp; repeat from * 2 more times; repeat between [ ], join, **do not** turn, fasten off.

Rnd 9: Join aqua with sc in first sc, [◊*ch 2, (sc, ch 2, sc) in ch sp of next shell, ch 2, sc in next sc; repeat from * across to next corner, ch 2, skip next dc, (sc, ch 2, sc) in next dc, ch 2, skip next dc, (sc, ch 3, sc) in next corner ch-3 sp, ch 2, skip next dc, (sc, ch 2, sc) in next dc, ch 2, skip next dc◊, sc in next sc]; repeat between [ ] 2 more times; repeat between ◊◊, join, fasten off.✤

BLOCK DIAGRAM

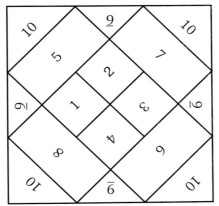

ASSEMBLY DIAGRAM

Sweet Dreams

Joyfully celebrate the arrival of your precious bundle of joy with a lovingly crafted blanket befitting the occasion. Long considered the gift of choice when heralding life's most glorious event, baby afghans are a gift that keeps on giving for generations to come.

Baby Aran

erma fielder, designer

Dress up your nursery with this classic aran enhanced with puff stitches. Made in sparkling baby pompadour, it's sure to be a treasured keepsake.

Finished Size
31¼" x 35"

Materials
Baby pompadour yarn — 19½ oz. white; G crochet hook or size needed to obtain gauge.

Gauge
4 sc sts = 1"; 5 sc rows = 1".

Skill Level
★★ Average

Instructions

Afghan

Row 1: Ch 122, sc in 2nd ch from hook, sc in each ch across, turn (121 sc).

Note: For **puff stitch (puff st)**, yo, insert hook in next st, yo, draw up ½"-long lp, (yo, insert hook in same st, yo, draw up ½"-long lp) 3 times, yo, draw through all 9 lps on hook.

Row 2: Ch 1, sc in first 4 sts, puff st, (sc in next 15 sts, puff st) 7 times, sc in last 4 sts, turn (113 sc, 8 puff sts).

Notes: For **front post stitch (fp)** *(see fig. 9, pg. 159)*, yo, insert hook from front to back around post of next st on row before last, complete as dc. Skip next st on last row behind post st.

For **front post cluster (fp cl),** yo, insert hook from front to back around post of next st on row before last, yo, draw lp through, yo, draw through 2 lps on hook, yo, insert hook around same st, yo, draw lp through, yo, draw through 2 lps on hook, yo, draw through all 3 lps on hook. Skip next st on last row behind fp cl.

Row 3: Ch 1, sc in each of first 2 sts, (fp, sc in each of next 3 sts, fp, sc in next 4 sts, fp cl, sc in next st, fp cl, sc in next 4 sts) 7 times, fp, sc in each of next 3 sts, fp, sc in each of last 2 sts, turn.

Row 4: Ch 1, sc in each of first 3 sts, (puff st, sc in next st, puff st, sc in next 13 sts) 7 times, puff st, sc in next st, puff st, sc in each of last 3 sts, turn.

Row 5: Ch 1, sc in each of first 2 sts, (fp around next fp on row before last, sc in each of next 3 sts, fp around next fp, sc in each of next 3 sts, fp cl around next fp cl on row before last, sc in each of next 3 sts, fp cl around next fp cl, sc in each of next 3 sts) 7 times, fp around next fp, sc in each of next 3 sts, fp around next fp, sc in each of last 2 sts, turn.

Row 6: Repeat row 2.

Row 7: Ch 1, sc in each of first 2 sts, (fp around next fp, sc in each of next 3 sts, fp around next fp, sc in each of next 2 sts, fp cl around next fp cl, sc in next 5 sts, fp cl around next fp cl, sc in each of next 2 sts) 7 times, fp around next fp, sc in each of next 3 sts, fp around next fp, sc in each of last 2 sts, turn.

Row 8: Repeat row 4.

Note: For **popcorn stitch (pc)**, 4 dc in next st, drop lp from hook, insert hook in first st of 4-dc group, pick up dropped lp, draw through st.

Row 9: Ch 1, sc in each of first 2 sts, (fp around next fp, sc in each of next 3 sts, fp around next fp, sc in next st, fp cl around next

Continued on page 67

Blue Gingham

elizabeth a. white, designer

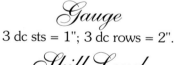

Baby and teddy will snuggle warmly beneath this tranquil checkered blanket. Restful shades of blue, worked in easy double crochet, will make this one a favorite for gift-giving.

Finished Size
38½" square

Materials
Worsted-weight yarn — 14 oz. lt. blue, 8 oz. each dk. blue and white; I crochet hook or size needed to obtain gauge.

Gauge
3 dc sts = 1"; 3 dc rows = 2".

Skill Level
★ Easy

Instructions
Afghan
Note: When changing colors *(see fig. 12, pg. 159),* work over dropped color and pick up as needed.

Row 1: With dk. blue, ch 112, dc in 4th ch from hook, dc in next 8 chs changing to lt. blue in last st made, (dc in next 10 chs changing to dk. blue in last st made, dc in next 10 chs changing to lt. blue in last st made) 4 times, dc in next 10 chs changing to dk. blue in last st made, dc in last 10 chs, turn.

Rows 2-5: Ch 3, dc in next 9 sts changing to lt. blue in last st made, (dc in next 10 sts changing to dk. blue in last st made, dc in next 10 sts changing to lt. blue in last st made) 4 times, dc in next 10 sts changing to dk. blue in last st made, dc in last 10 sts, turn. At end of last row, fasten off.

Row 6: Join lt. blue with sl st in first st, ch 3, dc in next 9 sts changing to white in last st made, (dc in next 10 sts changing to lt. blue in last st made, dc in next 10 sts changing to white in last st made) 4 times, dc in next 10 sts changing to lt. blue in last st made, dc in last 10 sts, turn.

Rows 7-10: Ch 3, dc in next 9 sts changing to white in last st made, (dc in next 10 sts changing to lt. blue in last st made, dc in next 10 sts changing to white in last st made) 4 times, dc in next 10 sts changing to lt. blue in last st made, dc in last 10 sts, turn. At end of last row, fasten off.

Row 11: Join dk. blue with sl st in first st, ch 3, dc in next 9 sts changing to lt. blue in last st made, (dc in next 10 sts changing to dk. blue in last st made, dc in next 10 sts changing to lt. blue in last st made) 4 times, dc in next 10 sts changing to dk. blue in last st made, dc in last 10 sts, turn.

Rows 12-15: Repeat rows 2-5.

Rows 16-55: Repeat rows 6-15 consecutively. At end of last row, **do not** turn or fasten off.

Border
Rnd 1: Working around outer edge, 2 sc in end of each row and sc in each st around with 3 sc in each corner st, join with sl st in first sc.

Rnds 2-3: Ch 1, sc in each st around with 3 sc in each center corner st, join. At end of last rnd, fasten off.❖

Circus Fun

jo ann maxwell, designer

Strike up the band, bring in the clowns! This colorful throw with bold cables and bright popcorns will transform your child's room into a circus of fun.

Finished Size
38" x 39"

Materials
Worsted-weight yarn — 8 oz. white, 2 oz. each red, purple, turquoise and yellow, 1½ oz. orange, 1 oz. each green and pink; I crochet hook or size needed to obtain gauge.

Gauge
3 dc sts = 1"; 3 dc rows = 2".

Skill Level
★★ Average

Instructions
Afghan

Row 1: With white, ch 108, sc in 2nd ch from hook, sc in each ch across, drop lp from hook, turn (107 sc).

Row 2: Join red with sc in first st, (ch 3, skip next 2 unworked sts, sc in next st, **turn,** sc in each of next 3 chs, sl st in next st, **turn,** ch 1; working behind ch lp, sc in next skipped st, 2 sc in next skipped st) across to last st, sc in last st, fasten off red, **do not** turn.

Row 3: Pick up white, sl st in same st as first sl st, ch 3, (dc in each of next 2 sts, dc in same st as next sl st) across to last 4 sts, dc in last 4 sts, turn (107 dc).

Row 4: Ch 3, dc in next st, (ch 1, skip next st, dc in each of next 2 sts) across, turn.

Row 5: Ch 3, dc in each st and in each ch sp across, **do not** turn, fasten off.

Notes: For **popcorn (pc)**, 5 dc in next st changing to white in last st made, drop lp from hook, insert hook in first st of 5-dc group, pick up dropped lp, draw through st.

When changing colors *(see fig. 12, pg. 159)*, work over dropped color and pick up as needed.

Row 6: Join white with sl st in first st, ch 3, dc in next st changing to yellow, pc, (dc in next 5 sts changing to yellow in last st made, pc) across to last 2 sts, dc in each of last 2 sts, fasten off yellow, turn.

Row 7: Ch 3, dc in each st across, turn.

Row 8: Ch 3, dc in next st, (ch 1, skip next st, dc in each of next 2 sts) across, turn.

Row 9: Ch 3, dc in each st and in each ch sp across, turn, drop lp from hook.

Row 10: With turquoise, repeat row 2.

Rows 11-13: Repeat rows 3-5.

Row 14: Substituting orange for yellow, repeat row 6.

Rows 15-17: Repeat rows 7-9.

Row 18: With purple, repeat row 2.

Rows 19-25: Repeat rows 3-9.

Row 26: With green, repeat row 2.

Rows 27-29: Repeat rows 3-5.

Row 30: Substituting orange for yellow, repeat row 6

Rows 31-33: Repeat rows 7-9.

Row 34: With pink, repeat row 2.

Rows 35-41: Repeat rows 3-9.

Row 42: With purple, repeat row 2.

Rows 43-45: Repeat rows 3-5.

Row 46: Substituting orange for yellow, repeat row 6.

Rows 47-49: Repeat rows 7-9.

Row 50: With turquoise, repeat row 2.

Rows 51-57: Repeat rows 3-9.

Continued on page 67

Pastel Clouds

aline suplinskas, designer

This contemporary ripple worked in soft pastels will complement any nursery. Made with easy-care washable baby yarn, it's reversible and a wonderful project for beginners.

Finished Size
36¼" x 40"

Materials
Baby pompadour yarn — 3½ oz. each green, pink, blue and yellow; F crochet hook or size needed to obtain gauge.

Gauge
5 sts = 1"; 2 dc rows and 2 sc rows = 1¼".

Skill Level
★ Easy

Instructions
Afghan

Row 1: With green, ch 241, sc in 2nd ch from hook, sc in each of next 3 chs, 3 sc in next ch, sc in next 4 chs, (skip next 2 chs, sc in next 4 chs, 3 sc in next ch, sc in next 4 chs) across, turn (242 sc).

Note: Work remaining rows in **back lps** *(see fig. 1, pg. 158).*

Row 2: Ch 3, dc next 2 sts tog, dc in each of next 2 sts, 3 dc in next st, dc in next 4 sts, (skip next 2 sts, dc in next 4 sts, 3 dc in next st, dc in next 4 sts) 20 times, skip next 2 sts, dc in next 4 sts, 3 dc in next st, dc in each of next 3 sts, dc last 2 sts tog, turn.

Row 3: Ch 1, sc in first st, sc next 2 sts tog, sc in each of next 2 sts, 3 sc in next st, sc in next 4 sts, (skip next 2 sts, sc in next 4 sts, 3 sc in next st, sc in next 4 sts) 20 times, skip next 2 sts, sc in next 4 sts, 3 sc in next st, sc in each of next 3 sts, sc last 2 sts tog, turn.

Row 4: Ch 3, dc next 2 sts tog, dc in each of next 2 sts, 3 dc in next st, dc in next 4 sts, (skip next 2 sts, dc in next 4 sts, 3 dc in next st, dc in next 4 sts) 20 times, skip next 2 sts, dc in next 4 sts, 3 dc in next st, dc in each of next 3 sts, dc last 2 sts tog, turn, fasten off.

Row 5: Join yellow with sc in first st, sc next 2 sts tog, sc in each of next 2 sts, 3 sc in next st, sc in next 4 sts, (skip next 2 sts, sc in next 4 sts, 3 sc in next st, sc in next 4 sts) 20 times, skip next 2 sts, sc in next 4 sts, 3 sc in next st, sc in each of next 3 sts, sc last 2 sts tog, turn.

Rows 6-8: Repeat rows 2-4.

Rows 9-116: Following color sequence of blue, pink, green, yellow, repeat rows 5-8 consecutively, ending with green. At end of last row, **do not** fasten off.

Row 117: Repeat row 3, fasten off.✤

Razzle Dazzle

katherine eng, designer

Baby will coo with delight as he settles down for a nap beneath these eye-catching stripes. Made of worsted-weight yarn, this light and airy design is sure to keep the chill off.

Finished Size
36" x 40"

Materials
Worsted-weight yarn — 14 oz. lt. green, 8½ oz. lavender and 6½ oz. yellow; H crochet hook or size needed to obtain gauge.

Gauge
7 sc sts = 2"; 7 sc rows = 2".

Skill Level
★★ Average

Instructions

Center

Row 1: With lt. green, ch 14, sc in 2nd ch from hook, sc in each ch across, turn (13 sc).

Note: For **shell,** (2 dc, ch 2, 2 dc) in next st.

Row 2: Ch 3, 2 dc in same st, skip next 2 sts, sc in next st, skip next 2 sts, shell in next st, skip next 2 sts, sc in next st, skip next 2 sts, 3 dc in last st, turn (6 dc, 2 sc, 1 shell).

Row 3: Ch 1, sc in first st, shell in next sc, sc in ch sp of next shell, shell in next sc, sc in last dc, turn (3 sc, 2 shells). Front of row 3 is right side of work.

Row 4: Ch 3, 2 dc in same st, sc in next shell, shell in next sc, sc in next shell, 3 dc in last st, turn.

Row 5: Ch 1, sc in each of first 2 dc, hdc in next dc, dc in next sc, hdc in next dc, sc in next dc, sc in next ch sp, sc in next dc, hdc in next dc, dc in next sc, hdc in next dc, sc in each of last 2 dc, turn (13 sts).

Row 6: Ch 1, sc in first st, (ch 1, skip next st, sc in next st) across, fasten off.

Row 7: With wrong side facing you, working in starting ch on opposite side of row 1, join with sl st in first ch, ch 3, 2 dc in same ch, skip next 2 chs, sc in next ch, skip next 2 chs, shell in next ch, skip next 2 chs, sc in next ch, skip next 2 chs, 3 dc in last ch, turn (6 dc, 2 sc, 1 shell).

Rows 8-11: Repeat rows 3-6. At end of last row, **do not** fasten off, turn.

Rnd 12: Working around outer edge, ch 1, *(sc, ch 2, sc) in first st, sc in each ch sp and in each st across with (sc, ch 2, sc) in last st, skip first row, sc in end of each sc row and 3 sc in end of each dc row across to last row, skip last row; repeat from * one more time, join with sl st in first sc, fasten off (13 sc on each short end, 19 sc on each long edge, 4 ch-2 sps).

Strips No. 1 & 2

Row 1: With right side facing you, working on one long edge, join yellow with sc in corner ch-2 sp, ch 1, skip next st, (sc in next st, ch 1, skip next st) across to next corner ch-2 sp, sc in ch sp leaving remaining sts unworked, turn.

Rows 2-6: Ch 1, sc in first st, (ch 1, skip next ch sp, sc in next st) across, turn. At end of last row, fasten off.

Repeat on opposite long edge.

Strips No. 3 & 4

Row 1: With right side facing you, working on one short end and across ends of rows on Strips, join lavender with sc in first row, ch 1, skip next row, (sc in next row, ch 1, skip next row) 2 times, sc in next ch-2 sp, ch 1, skip

Continued on page 66

Continued from page 64

next st, (sc in next st, ch 1, skip next st) across to next ch-2 sp, sc in next ch sp, (ch 1, skip next row, sc in next row) across, turn.

Rows 2-6: Repeat rows 2-6 of Strips No. 1 & 2.

Repeat on opposite short end.

Border No. 1

Note: You should always have an odd number of sts between corner ch-2 sps.

Rnd 1: With right side facing you, join lt. green with sc in top right-hand corner st on one short end, ch 2, sc in same st, *sc in each ch sp and in each st across to next corner st, (sc, ch 2, sc) in next corner st; working in ends of rows on Strip, skip first row, sc in next 5 rows, sc in each st and in each ch sp across to ends of rows on next Strip, sc in first 5 rows, skip last row*, (sc, ch 2, sc) in next corner st; repeat between **, join with sl st in first sc, **turn.**

Rnd 2: Sl st in next st, ch 1, sc in same st, *ch 1, skip next st, (sc in next st, ch 1, skip next st) across to next ch-2 sp, (sc, ch 2, sc) in next ch-2 sp; repeat from * 3 more times, ch 1, skip last st, join with sl st in first sc, **turn.**

Rnd 3: Ch 1, sc in each st and in each ch-1 sp around with (sc, ch 2, sc) in each corner ch-2 sp, fasten off.

Strips No. 5 & 6

Working on short ends, work same as Strips No. 1 & 2.

Strips No. 7 & 8

Working on long edges, work same as Strips No. 3 & 4.

Border No. 2

Joining in lower right-hand corner, work same as Border No. 1.

Strips No. 9-12

Work same as Strips No. 1-4.

Border No. 3

Work same as Border No. 1.

Strips No. 13 & 14

Working on short ends, work same as Strips No. 1 & 2.

Strips No. 15 & 16

Working on long edges, work same as Strips No. 3 & 4.

Border No. 4

Joining in lower right-hand corner, work same as Border No. 1.

Strips No. 17-20

Work same as Strips No. 1-4.

Border No. 5

Rnds 1-3: Repeat rnds 1-3 of Border No. 1.

Rnd 4: Join yellow with sc in any corner ch sp, ch 2, sc in same sp, *[ch 1, skip next st, (sc in next st, ch 1, skip next st) across to next corner] ch-2 sp, (sc, ch 2, sc) in next ch sp; repeat from * 2 more times; repeat between [ ], join with sl st in first sc.

Rnd 5: Sl st in next corner ch sp, ch 1, (sc, ch 2, sc) in same sp, sc in each st and in each ch-1 sp around with (sc, ch 2, sc) in each corner ch sp, join, fasten off (107 sc on each short end, 113 sc on each long edge).

Rnd 6: Join lt. green with sc in 3rd sc after any corner ch sp, *[skip next 2 sts, (shell in next st, skip next 2 sts, sc in next st, skip next 2 sts) across to next corner ch sp, (3 dc, ch 2, 3 dc) in next corner ch sp, skip next 2 sts], sc in next st; repeat from * 2 more times; repeat between [ ], join, **turn.**

Rnd 7: Ch 3, (dc, ch 2, 2 dc) in same st, *[skip next dc, sc in next dc, skip next dc, (3 dc, ch 2, 3 dc) in next corner ch sp, skip next dc, sc in next dc, skip next dc], shell in next sc, (sc in ch sp of next shell, shell in next sc) across to next corner; repeat from * 2 more times; repeat between [ ], (shell in next sc, sc in ch sp of next shell) across, join with sl st in top of ch-3, **turn.**

Rnd 8: Sl st in next sc, ch 3, *(shell in next shell, dc in next sc) across to next corner, skip next dc, shell in next dc, skip next dc, (sc, ch 3, sc) in next corner ch sp, skip next dc, shell in next dc, skip next dc, dc in next sc; repeat from * 3 more times, shell in next shell, join, **do not** turn.

Rnd 9: Ch 1, sc in each sc and in each dc around with (sc, ch 2, sc) in each ch-2 sp of each shell and (sc, ch 3, sc) in each corner ch-3 sp, join, fasten off.

Rnd 10: Join lavender with sc in any corner ch-3 sp, ch 3, sc in same sp, [◊ch 2, skip next 2 sts, sc in next st, ch 2, skip next 2 sts, (sc, ch 2, sc) in next ch-2 sp, *ch 2, skip next 3 sts, sc in next st, ch 2, skip next 3 sts, (sc, ch 2, sc) in next ch-2 sp; repeat from * across to 5 sts before next corner ch-3 sp, ch 2, skip next 2 sts, sc in next st, ch 2, skip next 2 sts◊, (sc, ch 3, sc) in next corner ch sp]; repeat between [ ] 2 more times; repeat between ◊◊, join, fasten off.

Rnd 11: Join lt. green with sc in any corner ch-3 sp, ch 3, sc in same sp, [◊ch 2, sc in next sc, *ch 2, skip next ch-2 sp and next sc, (sc, ch 2, sc) in next ch-2 sp, ch 2, skip next ch-2 sp, sc in next sc; repeat from * across to next corner, ch 2, skip next ch-2 sp◊, (sc, ch 3, sc) in next corner ch sp; repeat between [ ] 2 times; repeat between ◊◊, join, **turn,** fasten off.

Rnd 12: Join lavender with sl st in any cor-
ner ch-3 sp, ch 3, (sl st, ch 4, sl st, ch 3, sl st) in same ch sp, [◊ch 2, skip next ch sp, (sl st, ch 4, sl st) in next sc, ch 2, skip next ch sp and next sc, (sl st, ch 3, sl st) in next ch sp, *ch 2, skip next ch sp, (sl st, ch 3, sl st) in next sc, ch 2, skip next ch sp and next sc, (sl st, ch 3, sl st) in next ch sp; repeat from * across to sc before next corner, ch 2, (sc, ch 4, sc) in next sc, ch 2◊, (sl st, ch 3, sl st, ch 4, sl st, ch 3, sl st) in next corner ch sp]; repeat between [ ] 2 times; repeat between ◊◊, join with sl st in joining sl st, fasten off.✿

Baby Aran

Continued from page 57

fp cl, sc in each of next 3 sts, pc in next st, sc in each of next 3 sts, fp cl around next fp cl, sc in next st) 7 times, fp around next fp, sc in each of next 3 sts, fp around next fp, sc in each of last 2 sts, turn.

Row 10: Repeat row 2.

Row 11: Repeat row 7.

Rows 12-13: Repeat rows 4 and 5.

Row 14: Repeat row 2.

Row 15: Ch 1, sc in each of first 2 sts, (fp around next fp, sc in each of next 3 sts, fp around next fp, sc in next 4 sts, fp cl around next fp cl, sc in next st, fp cl around next fp cl, sc in next 4 sts) 7 times, fp around next fp, sc in each of next 3 sts, fp around next fp, sc in each of last 2 sts, turn.

Rows 16-171: Repeat rows 4-15 consecutively.

Row 172: Ch 1, sc in each st across, turn.

Rnd 173: Working around outer edge, ch 3, 3 dc in same st, drop lp from hook, insert hook in top of ch-3, pick up dropped lp, draw through ch, ch 3, pc in same st, sc in each of next 3 sts, (pc in next st, sc in each of next 3 sts) across with (pc, ch 3, pc) in last st; *working in ends of rows, skip first row, sc in each of next 3 rows, (pc in next row, sc in each of next 3 rows) across*; working in starting ch on opposite side of row 1, (pc, ch 3, pc) in first ch, sc in each of next 3 chs, (pc, sc in each of next 3 chs) across with (pc, ch 3, pc) in last ch; repeat between **, join with sl st in first sc, fasten off.✿

Circus Fun

Continued from page 61

Row 58: With red, repeat row 2.

Row 59: Pick up white, ch 1, sc in same st as first sl st, (sc in each of next 2 sts, sc in same st as next sl st) across to last 4 sts, sc in last 4 sts, **do not** turn (107 sc).

Note: For **shell,** (2 dc, ch 2, 2 dc) in end of next row.

Rnd 60: Working in ends of rows, sl st in
top of next dc row, ch 3, (dc, ch 2, 2 dc) in top of same row, 2 dc in same row, *shell in next dc row, (skip next dc row, shell in next dc row) 23 times, 2 dc in next dc row, skip next sc row, shell in last sc row*; working in starting ch on opposite side of row 1, dc in each ch across, shell in first sc row, 2 dc in next dc row; repeat between **, dc in each st across, join with sl st in top of ch-3, fasten off.✿

Shades of Beauty

A vibrant symphony of expressive hues and subtle tints combine in a spontaneous medley of exhilarating designs to set your soul soaring and pulse racing. Treat yourself to a bouquet of inviting richness and color that will capture your heart and delight your senses.

Strawberry Sundae

sandra miller-maxfield, designer

Delicate shades of pink cascade gorgeously across this alluring afghan. Pretty puff stitches and groups of double crochet add attractive dimension to this enchanting design.

Finished Size
48½" x 65" without fringe

Materials
Worsted-weight yarn — 27 oz. dark rose, 23 oz. med. rose and 19 oz. lt. rose; tapestry needle; H crochet hook or size needed to obtain gauge.

Gauge
1 puff st = 1". Each Strip is 4" wide.

Skill Level
★ Easy

Instructions
Strip (make 12)
Note: For **puff stitch (ps)**, yo, insert hook in next ch sp, yo, draw up long lp, (yo, insert hook in same sp, yo, draw up long lp) 3 times, yo, draw through all 9 lps on hook.

Row 1: With dk. rose, ch 4, sl st in first ch to form ring, ch 3, (ps, ch 2, ps, dc) in ring, turn (2 ps, 2 dc, 1 ch-2 sp).

Rows 2-70: Ch 3, (ps, ch 2, ps, dc) in next ch-2 sp, turn.

Row 71: Ch 3, (ps, ch 2, ps) in next ch-2 sp, ch 3, sl st in last st, fasten off.

Note: For **shell,** (3 dc, ch 3, 3 dc) in next row or ch sp.

Rnd 72: Working in ends of rows, join lt. rose with sl st in end of row 71, (ch 3, 2 dc, ch 3, 3 dc) in same row, 3 dc in each row across to last row, shell in last row, 3 dc in ring, shell in row 1, 3 dc in each row across to last row, shell in last row, 3 dc in ch-2 sp between ps, join with sl st in top of ch-3, fasten off.

Rnd 73: Join med. rose with sl st in ch sp of first shell, (ch 3, 2 dc, ch 3, 3 dc) in same sp; working in sps between 3-dc groups, *3 dc in each sp across to next shell, shell in ch sp of next shell, 3 dc in each of next 2 sps*, shell in ch sp of next shell; repeat between ** , join, fasten off.

Holding Strips wrong sides together, matching sts, working in **back lps** *(see fig. 1, pg. 158)* through both thicknesses, with med. rose, sew long edges together between ch-3 sps.

Edging
Join dk. rose with sc in any st, sc in each st, 2 sc in each ch-3 sp on each side of seams and 3 sc in each corner ch sp around, join with sl st in first sc, fasten off.

Fringe
For **each Fringe,** cut one strand of each color each 14" long. With all three strands held together, fold in half, insert hook in st, draw fold through st, draw all loose ends through fold, tighten. Trim ends.

Fringe in every other st on each short end of Afghan.✿

Autumn Glow

rosetta harshman, designer

As autumn breezes shuffle colorful leaves outside your windows, wrap up in this beautifully textured afghan. Luxurious fringe adds a lovely finishing touch.

Finished Size

47" x 69" without fringe

Materials

Worsted-weight yarn — 14 oz. each lt. brown and dk. brown, 13 oz. each ecru and rust; H crochet hook or size needed to obtain gauge.

Gauge

7 dc sts = 2"; 3 pattern rows = 2".

Skill Level

★ Easy

Instructions

Afghan

Notes: For **V-st,** (dc, ch 2, dc) in next st or sp.

For **dc next 3 chs or sts tog,** (yo, insert hook in next st, yo, draw lp through, yo, draw through 2 lps on hook) 3 times, yo, draw through all 4 lps on hook.

Row 1: With dk. brown, ch 137, dc in 4th ch from hook, dc in each of next 2 chs, (V-st in next ch, dc in next ch, dc next 3 chs tog, dc in next ch) 21 times, V-st in next ch, dc in last 4 chs, turn (22 V-sts, 71 dc).

Row 2: Ch 3, dc in next st, skip next st, dc in each of next 2 sts, (V-st in next ch-2 sp, dc in next st, dc next 3 sts tog, dc in next st) 21 times, V-st in next ch-2 sp, dc in each of next 2 sts, skip next st, dc in each of last 2 sts, turn, fasten off.

Row 3: Join lt. brown with sl st in first st, ch 3, dc in next st, skip next st, dc in each of next 2 sts, (V-st in next ch-2 sp, dc in next st, dc next 3 sts tog, dc in next st) 21 times, V-st in next ch-2 sp, dc in each of next 2 sts, skip next st, dc in each of last 2 sts, turn.

Row 4: Repeat row 2.

Rows 5-6: With ecru, repeat rows 3 and 2.

Row 7: With rust, repeat row 3.

Rows 8-10: Repeat row 2, **do not** fasten off. At end of last row, fasten off.

Rows 11-12: With ecru, repeat rows 3 and 2.

Rows 13-14: With dk. brown, repeat rows 3 and 2.

Rows 15-100: Repeat rows 3-14 consecutively, ending with row 4.

Border

Rnd 1: Working around entire outer edge, join ecru with sl st in first st, ch 2, 2 hdc in same st, hdc in each st across to last st with 2 hdc in each ch-2 sp, 3 hdc in last st; working in ends of rows, 2 hdc in end of each row across; working in starting ch on opposite side of row 1, 3 hdc in first ch, hdc in each ch across to last ch with 2 hdc in ch at base of each V-st, 3 hdc in last ch, 2 hdc in end of each row across, join with sl st in top of ch-2, fasten off.

Rnd 2: Join lt. brown with sl st in any st, ch 3, dc in each st around with 3 dc in each center corner st, join, fasten off.

Rnd 3: Join dk. brown with sl st in first of any 3-dc corner group, ch 2, dc in same st, 3 dc in next st, 2 dc in next st, (dc in each st across to next 3-dc corner group, 2 dc in next st, 3 dc in next st, 2 dc in next st) 3 times, dc in each st across, join, fasten off.

Fringe

For **each Fringe,** cut 6 strands each 16" long. With all strands held together, fold in half, insert hook in st, draw fold through, draw all loose ends through fold, tighten. Trim ends.

Alternating lt. brown and dk. brown, Fringe every third st on each short end of afghan.

Desert Flower

katherine eng, designer

Soft neutral shades ripple like shifting sands around a lovely field of blossoms. Elegant and decorative, this afghan will make a stunning complement to any room.

Finished Size
47½" x 62½"

Materials
Worsted-weight yarn — 24½ oz. tan, 19½ oz. white and 12½ oz. off-white; tapestry needle; F crochet hook or size needed to obtain gauge.

Gauge
Rnds 1-3 = 2½" across.
Each Block is 7½" square.

Skill Level
★★ Average

Instructions

Block (make 35)
Center
Note: For **beginning cluster (beg cl),** ch 3, (yo, insert hook in ring, yo, draw lp through, yo, draw through 2 lps on hook) 2 times, yo, draw through all 3 lps on hook.

For **cluster (cl),** (yo, insert hook in ring, yo, draw lp through, yo, draw through 2 lps on hook) 3 times, yo, draw through all 4 lps on hook.

Rnd 1: With tan, ch 4, sl st in first ch to form ring, beg cl, ch 4, (cl, ch 4) 5 times, join with sl st in top of first cl (6 cls, 6 ch sps).

Rnd 2: Sl st in next ch sp, ch 1, 4 sc in same ch sp, ch 1, (4 sc in next ch sp, ch 1) around, join with sl st in first sc (24 sc, 6 ch sps).

Rnd 3: Ch 1, sc in each st and 2 sc in each ch sp around, join (36).

Rnd 4: Ch 1, sc in each of first 3 sts, *[hdc in next st, dc in next st, (2 dc, ch 2, 2 dc) in next st, dc in next st, hdc in next st], sc in next 4 sts; repeat from * 2 more times; repeat between [ ], sc in last st, join.

Rnd 5: Ch 1, sc in each st around with (sc, ch 3, sc) in each ch-2 sp, join, fasten off.

Section No. 1
Row 1: With right side facing you, join white with sc in any ch-3 sp (see Block Diagram on pg. 77), sc in next 7 sts leaving remaining sts unworked, turn (8 sc).

Rows 2-3: Ch 1, sc first 2 sts tog, sc in each st across to last 2 sts, sc last 2 sts tog, turn (6, 4).

Row 4: Ch 1, sc first 2 sts tog, sc last 2 sts tog, turn (2).

Row 5: Ch 1, sc next 2 sts tog, fasten off.
Repeat Section No. 1 on remaining three sides of Center.

Section No. 2
Row 1: With right side facing you, join white with sc in first unworked st on Center after any Section No. 1 (see Block Diagram), sc in next 6 sts, sc in next ch-3 sp, turn (8 sc).

Rows 2-5: Repeat same rows of Section No. 1.
Repeat Section No. 2 on remaining three sides of Center.

Section No. 3
Note: Sl sts are not used or counted as sts.

Row 1: With right side facing you, join off-white with sc in end of last row on any Section No. 1, evenly space 5 more sc across ends of next 4 rows, sl st in end of first row on Section No. 2, sl st in end of next row, turn (6 sc).

Row 2: Ch 1, sc in each st across, turn.

Continued on page 76

Desert Flower

Continued from page 75

Row 3: Ch 1, sc in each st across, sl st in end of rows 2 and 3 on Section No. 2, turn.

Row 4: Ch 1, sc in each st across, turn.

Row 5: Ch 1, sc in each st across, sl st in end of rows 3 and 4 on Section No. 2, turn.

Row 6: Ch 1, sc in each st across, turn.

Row 7: Ch 1, sc in each st across, sl st in end of row 5 on Section No. 2, fasten off.

Repeat Section No. 3 on remaining three sides.

Edging

Rnd 1: With right side facing you, join tan with sc in any corner st, ch 2, sc in same corner, *[evenly space 23 sc across to next corner with hdc in Center ch-3 sp between Sections No. 2 and 1], (sc, ch 2, sc) in next corner; repeat from * 2 more times; repeat between [ ], join with sl st in first sc.

Rnd 2: Ch 1, sc in each st around with (sc, ch 3, sc) in each corner ch-2 sp, join, fasten off (28 sc on each edge between ch sps).

Holding Blocks wrong sides together, matching sts, working in **back lps** (see fig. 1, pg. 158) through both thicknesses, with tan, sew together in five rows of seven Blocks each.

Border

Rnd 1: With right side facing you, join tan with sc in any st, sc in each st, sc in each ch sp on each side of seams and hdc in each seam around with (sc, ch 3, sc) in each corner ch-3 sp, join with sl st in first sc (154 sts on each short end, 216 sts on each long edge, 4 ch-3 sps).

Rnd 2: Ch 1, sc in each st around with (sc, ch 3, sc) in each corner ch sp, join, fasten off.

Rnd 3: Join white with sc in any corner ch sp on one short end, ch 3, sc in same sp, *ch 2, skip next st, sc in next st, (ch 2, skip next 2 sts, sc in next st) across to one st before next corner ch sp, ch 2, skip next st, (sc, ch 3, sc) in next corner ch sp, ch 2, skip next 2 sts, (sc in next st, ch 2, skip next 2 sts) across to next corner*, (sc, ch 3, sc) in next corner ch sp; repeat between **, join.

Rnd 4: Sl st in next ch sp, ch 3, (2 dc, ch 2, 3 dc) in same sp, 3 dc in each ch-2 sp around with (3 dc, ch 2, 3 dc) in each corner ch sp, join with sl st in top of ch-3, **turn.**

Rnd 5: Sl st in each of next 2 sts, ch 1, sc in same st as last sl st, *(ch 2, sc in center st of next 3-dc group) across to next corner, ch 1, (sc, ch 3, sc) in next corner ch sp, ch 1, sc in center of next 3-dc group; repeat from * 3 more times, ch 2, join with sl st in first sc, **turn.**

Rnd 6: (Sl st, ch 3, 2 dc) in next ch-2 sp, 3 dc in each ch-2 sp around with 2 dc in each ch-1 sp and (2 dc, ch 2, 2 dc) in each corner ch sp, join with sl st in top of ch-3, **turn.**

Rnd 7: Sl st in each of next 2 sts, ch 1, sc in same st as last sl st, *[ch 2, skip next 2 sts, (sc in next st, ch 2, skip next 2 sts) across] to next corner ch sp, (sc, ch 3, sc) in corner ch sp; repeat from * 3 more times; repeat between [ ], join with sl st in first sc, **turn.**

Rnd 8: Sl st in next ch sp, ch 3, 2 dc in same sp, 3 dc in each ch-2 sp around with (3 dc, ch 2, 3 dc) in each corner ch sp, join with sl st in top of ch-3, **do not** turn.

Note: For **shell,** (2 dc, ch 2, 2 dc) in next st.

Rnd 9: (Sl st, ch 3, dc, ch 2, 2 dc) in next st, skip next 2 sts, sc in next st, skip next 2 sts, shell in next st, skip next 2 sts, sc in next st, *[(3 dc, ch 2, 3 dc) in next corner ch sp, skip next st, sc in next st, (skip next 2 sts, shell in next st, skip next 2 sts, sc in next st) across] to next corner; repeat from * 2 more times; repeat between [ ], join, **turn.**

Rnd 10: Sl st in next sc, *[ch 3, (sc, ch 3, sc) in ch sp of next shell, ch 3, sl st in next sc; repeat from * across to next corner, ch 4, (sc, ch 4, sc) in next corner ch sp, ch 4, sl st in next sc]; repeat between [ ] 3 more times, ch 3, (sc, ch 3, sc) in ch sp of next shell, ch 3, sl st in next sc, ch 3, (sc, ch 3, sc) in ch sp of next shell, ch 3, join with sl st in first sl st, **turn,** fasten off.

Rnd 11: Join off-white with sl st in any corner ch-4 sp, (ch 3, 4 dc, ch 2, 5 dc) in same ch sp, [◊ch 3, skip next 2 ch sps, (3 dc, ch 2, 3 dc) in next ch sp, *ch 1, skip next 2 ch sps, (3 dc, ch 2, 3 dc) in next ch sp; repeat from * across to 2 sps before next corner ch sp, ch 3, skip next 2 sps◊, (5 dc, ch 2, 5 dc) in next corner ch sp]; repeat between [ ] 2 more times; repeat between ◊◊, join with sl st in top of ch-3, **turn.**

Rnd 12: (Sl st, ch 1, sc, ch 3, sc) in next ch-3 sp, [◊ch 3, (sc, ch 3, sc) in next ch sp, *ch 3, sc in next ch-1 sp, ch 3, (sc, ch 3, sc) in next ch sp; repeat from * across to ch-3 sp before next corner, ch 3, (sc, ch 3, sc) in next ch-3 sp, ch 3, skip next 2 dc, sc in next dc, ch 3, skip next 2 dc, (sc, ch 3, sc) in next corner ch sp, ch 3, skip next 2 dc, sc in next dc, ch 3, skip next 2 dc◊, (sc, ch 3, sc) in next ch-3 sp]; repeat between [ ] 2 more times; repeat between ◊◊, join with sl st in first sc, **turn,** fasten off.

Rnd 13: Join tan with sc in any corner ch sp, (ch 3, sc, ch 5, sc, ch 3, sc) in same sp, [◊(ch 3, sc in next ch sp) 2 times, ch 3, (sc, ch 3, sc) in next ch sp, ch 3, skip next ch sp, (sc, ch 3, sc) in next ch sp, *ch 3, skip next ch sp, sc in next sc, ch 3, skip next ch sp, (sc, ch 3, sc) in next ch sp; repeat from * across to 4 ch sps before next corner ch sp, ch 3, skip next ch sp, (sc, ch 3, sc) in next ch sp, (ch 3, sc in next ch sp) 2 times, ch 3◊, (sc, ch 3, sc, ch 5, sc, ch 3, sc) in next corner ch sp]; repeat between [ ] 2 more times; repeat between ◊◊, join, fasten off.✣

Block Diagram

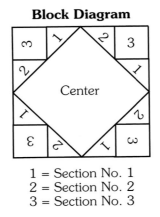

1 = Section No. 1
2 = Section No. 2
3 = Section No. 3

Ocean Waves

sandra miller-maxfield, designer

Sail off to adventure wrapped in this warm, nautical-look throw. Cheerful blue waves dance merrily across the surface of this purely ingenious design.

Finished Size
53" x 61½"

Materials
Worsted-weight yarn — 17 oz. lt. blue, 8½ oz. each med. blue and dk. blue; I crochet hook or size needed to obtain gauge.

Gauge
3 sts = 1"; 4 dc rows and 4 sc rows = 3½".

Skill Level
★ Easy

Instructions
Afghan

Row 1: With dk. blue, ch 161, dc in 4th ch from hook, dc in each ch across, turn (159 dc).

Row 2: Ch 1, sc in first 7 sts; (for **wave,** ch 7, 3 hdc in 3rd ch from hook, 3 hdc in each ch across; skip next st on last row, sc in next 7 sts) across, turn, fasten off.

Row 3: Join lt. blue with sl st in first st, ch 3, dc in next 6 sts; (working behind wave, dc in next skipped st on row before last, dc in next 7 sts) across, turn.

Row 4: Ch 1, sc in first 7 sts, *sc in next st and **back lp** (see fig. 1, pg. 158) of 12th st on next wave at same time, sc in next 7 sts; repeat from * across, turn.

Row 5: Ch 3, dc in each st across, turn.

Row 6: Ch 1, sc in each st across, turn.

Rows 7-9: Repeat rows 5 and 6 alternately, ending with row 5.

Row 10: Ch 1, sc in first 7 sts; (for **wave,** ch 7, 3 hdc in 3rd ch from hook, 3 hdc in each ch across; skip next st on last row, sc in next 7 sts) across, turn, fasten off.

Rows 11-140: Following color sequence of med. blue, lt. blue, dk. blue, lt. blue, repeat rows 3-10 consecutively, ending with row 4 and med. blue.✤

Shades of Green

dorris brooks, designer

A lacy medley of greens will capture your heart in this enticingly graceful afghan. You'll be eager to welcome spring with this fringed treasure.

Finished Size
46" x 65" without fringe

Materials
Worsted-weight yarn — 17½ oz. dk. green, 10½ oz. each med. green and lt. green; H crochet hook or size needed to obtain gauge.

Gauge
7 dc sts = 2"; 8 dc rows = 5".

Skill Level
★ Easy

Instructions
Afghan
Row 1: With dk. green, ch 163, dc in 4th ch from hook, dc in each ch across, turn (161 dc).

Note: For **V-stitch (V-st),** (dc, ch 2, dc) in next st.

Row 2: Ch 3, *dc in each of next 3 sts, V-st in next st, (skip next 4 sts, V-st in each of next 2 sts) 5 times, skip next 4 sts, V-st in next st; repeat from * 3 more times, dc in last 4 sts, turn.

Row 3: Ch 3, *dc in each of next 3 sts, V-st in first st of next V-st, (V-st in last st of next V-st, V-st in first st of next V-st) 5 times, V-st in last st of next V-st; repeat from * 3 more times, dc in last 4 sts, turn.

Rows 4-8: Ch 3, *dc in each of next 3 sts, V-st in first st of next V-st, (V-st in last st of next V-st, V-st in first st of next V-st) 5 times, V-st in last st of next V-st; repeat from * 3 more times, dc in last 4 sts, turn. At end of last row, fasten off.

Row 9: Join med. green with sl st in first st, repeat row 3.

Rows 10-16: Repeat row 3. At end of last row, fasten off.

Rows 17-104: Following color sequence of lt. green, dk. green, med. green, repeat rows 9-16 consecutively, ending with dk. green.

Fringe
For **each Fringe,** cut three strands of dk. green each 16" long. With all three strands held together, fold in half, insert hook in st, draw fold through, draw all loose ends through fold, tighten. Trim ends.

Fringe in every other st on each short end of afghan.❧

Country Charm

Americana at its best, the country look is one of spirited adventure mellowed by quiet character. With a sophistication all their own, these distinctive, yet touchable creations favor their surroundings with an unforgettable magic only country can bring.

Holiday Cranberry

nancy clevenger, designer

Cheerful holiday colors and perky berry stitches make this afghan the perfect room-brightener. The simple mile-a-minute styling makes it easy, too.

Finished Size
46" x 67"

Materials
Worsted-weight yarn — 20 oz. burgundy, 12 oz. off-white and 10 oz. dk. green; tapestry needle; J crochet hook or size needed to obtain gauge.

Gauge
3 dc sts = 1"; 2 dc rows = 1¼".

Skill Level
★★ Average

Instructions
Strip (make 9)
Note: For **berry stitch (bs),** insert hook in ch or st, yo, draw lp through, (yo, draw through one lp on hook) 4 times, yo, draw through both lps on hook.

Rnd 1: With burgundy, ch 173, sc in 2nd ch from hook, bs in next ch, (sc in next ch, bs in next ch) across, 3 sc in same ch as last st; working on opposite side of starting ch, bs in next ch, (sc in next ch, bs in next ch) across, 2 sc in same ch as last st, join with sl st in first sc (176 sc, 172 bs).

Rnd 2: Ch 1, bs in first sc, sc in next bs, (bs in next sc, sc in next bs) across to next 3-sc group, sc in next st, 3 sc in next st, sc in next st, sc in next bs, (bs in next sc, sc in next bs) across to next 2-sc group, sc in next st, 3 sc in last st, join with sl st in first bs (181 sc, 171 bs).

Rnd 3: Ch 1, sc in first 173 sts, 2 sc in next st, sc in next st, 2 sc in next st, sc in next 173 sts, 2 sc in next st, sc in next st, 2 sc in last st, join, fasten off (356 sc).

Rnd 4: Join green with sl st in first st, ch 3, dc in next 172 sts, 2 dc in each of next 2 sts, 3 dc in next st, 2 dc in each of next 2 sts, dc in next 173 sts, 2 dc in each of next 2 sts, 3 dc in next st, 2 dc in each of last 2 sts, join with sl st in top of ch-3, fasten off (368 dc).

Rnd 5: Join off-white with sl st in second st, ch 3, dc in same st, skip next st, (2 dc in next st, skip next st) 86 times, (3 dc in next st, skip next st) 4 times, (2 dc in next st, skip next st) 88 times, (3 dc in next st, skip next st) 4 times, 2 dc in next st, skip last st, join, fasten off.

With tapestry needle and off-white, working through **back lps** *(see fig. 1, pg. 158)* only, leaving 16 sts at each end of each Strip free, sew Strips together.

Border
Working around entire outer edge of afghan, join burgundy with sc in any st, (sl st, ch 3, sl st) in next st, *sc in next st, (sl st, ch 3, sl st) in next st; repeat from * around, join with sl st in first sc, fasten off.✿

Coral Blossoms

katherine eng, designer

Add a splash of color to your decor with this splendid example of old-fashioned elegance. Lacy floral motifs set together on point lend an adventurous note.

Finished Size
50" x 72"

Materials
Worsted-weight yarn — 25 oz. tan, 16 oz. off-white, 11 oz. coral; F crochet hook or size needed to obtain gauge.

Gauge
Rnds 1-3 of Square = 2½" across. Each Square is 7" x 7".

Skill Level
★★ Average

Instructions

Square No. 1

Rnd 1: With off-white, ch 4, sl st in first ch to form ring, ch 3, 15 dc in ring, join with sl st in top of ch-3, fasten off (16 dc).

Rnd 2: Working in spaces between dc, join tan with sc in any sp, ch 3, skip next 2 dc, (sc in next sp, ch 3, skip next 2 dc) around, join with sl st in first sc (8 ch sps, 8 sc).

Rnd 3: Ch 1, sc in first st, *[3 sc in next ch sp, (sc, ch 3, sc) in next st, 3 sc in next ch sp], sc in next st; repeat from * 2 more times;

repeat between [ ], join, fasten off (36 sc, 4 ch sps).

Rnd 4: Join coral with sc in second st after any corner ch sp, (*skip next 2 sts, 5 dc in next st, skip next 2 sts, sc in next st, skip next st, 5 dc in next corner ch sp, skip next st*, sc in next st) 3 times; repeat between **, join.

Rnd 5: Ch 3, sl st in same st, [*ch 3, skip next 2 dc, (sl st, ch 3, sl st) in next dc, ch 3, skip next 2 dc], (sl st, ch 3, sl st) in next sc; repeat from * 6 more times; repeat between [ ], join with sl st in joining sl st on previous rnd, fasten off.

Rnd 6: Join tan with sc in 4th ch sp after any corner ch sp, *[ch 1, skip next ch sp, 3 dc in next ch sp, ch 1, skip next ch sp, (3 dc, ch 2, 3 dc) in next corner ch sp, ch 1, skip next ch sp, 3 dc in next ch sp, ch 1, skip next ch sp], sc in next ch sp; repeat from * 2 more times; repeat between [ ], join with sl st in first sc.

Rnd 7: Ch 1, sc in each st and in each ch-1 sp around with (sc, ch 2, sc) in each corner ch sp, join, **turn,** fasten off (76 sc, 4 ch sps).

Rnd 8: Join off-white with sc in any corner ch sp, ch 3, sc in same sp, *[ch 1, skip next st, (sc in next st, ch 1, skip next st) across to next corner ch sp], (sc, ch 3, sc) in next corner ch sp; repeat from * 2 more times; repeat between [ ], join, **turn,** fasten off.

Rnd 9: Join tan with sc in any corner ch sp, ch 3, sc in same sp, *[ch 1, skip next st, (sc in next ch-1 sp, ch 1, skip next st) across to next corner ch sp], (sc, ch 3, sc) in next corner ch sp; repeat from * 2 more times; repeat between [ ], join, **do not** turn, fasten off.

Rnd 10: Join off-white with sc in any corner ch sp, ch 3, sc in same sp, *[ch 5, skip next 2 sc, (sc in next ch-1 sp, ch 5, skip next 2 sc) across to next corner ch sp], (sc, ch 3, sc) in next corner ch sp; repeat from * 2 more times; repeat between [ ], join, fasten off.

Square No. 2

Rnds 1-9: Repeat same rnds of Square No 1.
Notes: To **join ch lps,** drop lp from hook,

Continued on page 91

English Garden

katherine eng, designer

Crochet a lush, everblooming garden for your home in country blue and rich jeweltones. The neutral background makes it versatile as well as lovely.

Finished Size
43" x 57"

Materials
Worsted-weight yarn — 11 oz. off-white, 7 oz. lt. blue, 6 oz. white, 5½ oz. each tan and teal, 3½ oz. purple, 3 oz. lavender, 2 oz. bronze and 1½ oz. each dk. blue and burgundy; tapestry needle; F crochet hook or size needed to obtain gauge.

Gauge
Rnds 1-2 of Square = 2½" across.
Each Square is 6½" x 6½".

Skill Level
★★★ Challenging

Instructions

Square (make 35 — see note below)

Note: For rnd 5, make 8 squares using bronze, 8 squares using purple, 8 squares using lavender, 6 squares using dk. blue and 5 squares using burgundy.

Rnd 1: With white, ch 4, sl st in first ch to form ring, ch 1, 8 sc in ring, join with sl st in first sc (8 sc).

Notes: **For beginning dc cluster (beg dc cl),** yo, insert hook in next st, yo, draw lp through, yo, draw through 2 lps on hook, yo, insert hook in same st, yo, draw lp through, yo, draw through 2 lps on hook, yo, draw through all 3 lps on hook.

For **dc cluster (dc cl),** yo, insert hook in next st, yo, draw lp through, yo, draw through 2 lps on hook, (yo, insert hook in same st, yo, draw lp through, yo, draw through 2 lps on hook) 2 times, yo, draw through all 4 lps on hook.

Rnd 2: Ch 3, beg cl in same st, ch 3, (cl in next st, ch 3) around, join with sl st in top of beg cl, fasten off (8 cls, 8 ch sps).

Note: For **tr cluster (tr cl),** yo 2 times, insert hook in ch sp, yo, draw lp through, (yo, draw through 2 lps on hook) 2 times, yo 2 times, insert hook in same ch sp, yo, draw lp through, (yo, draw through 2 lps on hook) 2 times, yo, draw through all 3 lps on hook.

Rnd 3: Join lt. blue with sl st in any ch sp, (ch 4, tr cl, ch 4, sl st) in same sp, ch 1, *(sl st, ch 4, tr cl, ch 4, sl st) in next ch sp, ch 1; repeat from * around, join with sl st in first sl st, fasten off.

Rnd 4: Join teal with sc in any ch-1 sp, ch 4, skip next ch-4, (sl st, ch 3, sl st) in top of next tr cl, ch 4, *sc in next ch-1 sp, ch 4, skip next ch-4, (sl st, ch 3, sl st) in top of next cl, ch 4; repeat from * around, join with sl st in first sc, fasten off.

Rnd 5: Join designated color (see beginning Note) with sc in any ch-3 sp, ch 2, (tr, ch 1, tr) in **back lp** *(see fig. 1, pg. 158)* of next sc, ch 2, *sc in next ch-3 sp, ch 2, (tr, ch 1, tr) in **back lp** of next sc, ch 2; repeat from * around, join, fasten off.

Rnd 6: Join off-white with sc in any sc, *[2 sc in next ch-2 sp, sc in next tr, hdc in next ch-1 sp, dc in next tr, 2 dc in next ch-2 sp, (2 tr, ch 3, 2 tr) in next sc, 2 dc in next ch-2 sp, dc in next tr, hdc in next ch-1 sp, sc in next tr, 2 sc in next ch-2 sp], sc in next sc; repeat from * 2 more times; repeat between [ ], join (76 sts,

Continued on page 90

English Garden

Continued from page 89

4 ch-3 sps).

Rnd 7: Ch 1, sc in each st around with (sc, ch 3, sc) in each ch-3 sp, join, fasten off (84 sc, 4 ch-3 sps).

Rnd 8: Join tan with sc in any ch sp, ch 3, sc in same sp, *[ch 1, skip next st, (sc in next st, ch 1, skip next st) across to next corner ch sp], (sc, ch 3, sc) in next sp; repeat from * 2 more times; repeat between [ ], join, fasten off.

With tapestry needle and tan, working in **back lps** only, sew Squares together in five rows of seven blocks each according to Assembly Diagram.

Border

Rnd 1: Join tan with sc in first st after any corner ch-3 sp, sc in each ch sp, sc in each st, hdc in each ch-3 sp on each side of seams and hdc in each seam around with (sc, ch 3, sc) in each corner ch sp, join, **turn** (129 sts on each short end, 181 sts on each long edge, 4 ch-3 sps).

Rnd 2: Ch 1, sc in first st, skip next st, (sc, ch 3, sc) in next corner ch sp, *[ch 1, skip next st, (sc in next st, ch 1, skip next st) across to next corner], (sc, ch 3, sc) in next corner ch sp; repeat from * 2 more times; repeat between [ ], join, **turn,** fasten off.

ASSEMBLY DIAGRAM

E	C	B	C	E
B	A	D	A	B
A	D	C	D	A
C	B	E	B	C
A	D	C	D	A
B	A	D	A	B
E	C	B	C	E

A = Rnd 5 is bronze
B = Rnd 5 is purple
C = Rnd 5 is lavender
D = Rnd 5 is dk. blue
E = Rnd 5 is burgundy

Rnd 3: Join lavender with sl st in first ch-1 sp after any corner, ch 4, (dc, ch 1) in each ch sp around with (2 dc, ch 2, 2 dc, ch 1) in each corner ch sp, join with sl st in 3rd ch of ch-4, **turn,** fasten off.

Rnd 4: Join white with sc in first ch-1 sp after any corner, *ch 1, (sc in next ch-1 sp, ch 1) across to next corner, skip next dc, sc in next dc, (sc, ch 3, sc) in next corner ch sp, sc in next dc; repeat from * 3 more times, ch 1, join with sl st in first sc, **turn.**

Rnd 5: Ch 3, dc in each ch-1 sp and in each st around with (2 dc, ch 3, 2 dc) in each corner ch sp, join with sl st in top of ch-3, **turn.**

Rnd 6: Sl st in next st, ch 1, sc in same st, *(ch 1, skip next st, sc in next st) across to next corner ch sp, (sc, ch 3, sc) in next sp, sc in next st; repeat from * 3 more times, (ch 1, skip next st, sc in next st) 2 times, ch 1, skip next st, join, **turn,** fasten off.

Rnd 7: Join purple with sl st in first ch-1 sp after any corner, ch 4, *(dc in next ch-1 sp, ch 1) across to next corner, skip next st, dc in next st, (2 dc, ch 2, 2 dc) in next ch sp, dc in next st, ch 1; repeat from * 3 more times, join with sl st in 3rd ch of ch-4, **turn,** fasten off.

Rnd 8: Join teal with sc in first ch-1 sp after any corner, ch 1, *(sc in next ch sp, ch 1) across to next corner, skip next dc, sc in next dc, ch 1, skip next dc, (sc, ch 3, sc) in next ch sp, ch 1, skip next dc, sc in next dc, ch 1; repeat from * 3 more times, join with sl st in first sc, **turn.**

Rnd 9: Ch 1, sc in each st and in each ch sp around with (sc, ch 3, sc) in each corner ch sp, join, **do not** turn, fasten off.

Note: For **shell,** (2 dc, ch 2, 2 dc) in next st.

Rnd 10: Join lt. blue with sc in 4th st after corner ch sp on one short end, [*skip next 2 sts, shell in next st, skip next 2 sts, sc in next st*; repeat between ** across to 3 sts before next corner ch sp, ch 1, skip next 3 sts, (3 dc, ch 2, 3 dc) in next ch sp, ch 1, skip next 2 sts, sc in next st; repeat between ** across to 2 sts before next corner ch sp, ch 1, skip next 2 sts, (3 dc, ch 2, 3 dc) in next ch sp, ch 1, skip next 3 sts], sc in next st; repeat between [ ], join, **do not** turn.

Rnd 11: Ch 1, sc in first st, [◊*ch 2, (sc, ch

2, sc) in ch sp of next shell, ch 2, sc in next sc; repeat from * across to next corner, ch 3, skip next dc, sc in next dc, ch 2, (sc, ch 2, sc) in next corner ch sp, ch 2, skip next dc, sc in next dc, ch 3, skip next dc◊, sc in next sc]; repeat between [ ] 2 more times; repeat between ◊◊, join, **turn,** fasten off.

Rnd 12: Join teal with sc in any corner ch sp, ch 3, sc in same sp, [◊ch 3, skip next ch sp, (sc, ch 2, sc) in next sc, ch 3, skip next ch sp, sc in next sc, *ch 2, skip next ch sp, (sc, ch 2, sc) in next ch sp, ch 2, skip next ch sp, sc in next sc; repeat from * across to 2 ch sps before next corner ch sp, ch 3, skip next ch sp, (sc, ch 2, sc) in next sc, ch 3, skip next ch sp◊, (sc, ch

3, sc) in next corner ch sp]; repeat between [ ] 2 more times; repeat between ◊◊, join, **turn,** fasten off.

Rnd 13: Join lt. blue with sl st in first ch sp after any corner ch sp, [◊ch 2, (sl st, ch 3, sl st) in next ch sp, ch 2, sl st in next ch sp, ch 1, sl st in next ch sp, *ch 3, (sl st, ch 3, sl st) in next ch sp, ch 3, sl st in next ch sp, ch 1, sl st in next ch sp; repeat from * across to 2 ch sps before next corner ch sp, ch 2, (sl st, ch 3, sl st) in next ch sp, ch 2, sl st in next ch sp, ch 2, (sl st, ch 3, sl st, ch 5, sl st, ch 3, sl st) in next corner ch sp, ch 2◊, sl st in next ch sp]; repeat between [ ] 2 more times; repeat between ◊◊, join with sl st in joining sl st, fasten off.✤

Coral Blossoms

Continued from page 86

insert hook from top to bottom through center ch of corresponding ch lp on other Square, pull dropped lp through.

When joining corners of more than two Squares, join through same ch as first joining.

Rnd 10: Join off-white with sc in any corner ch sp, ch 3, sc in same sp, *ch 5, skip next 2 sc, (sc in next ch-1 sp, ch 5, skip next 2 sc) across to next corner ch sp*, (sc, ch 3, sc) in next corner ch sp; repeat between **, sc in next corner ch sp, ch 1; joining to side of Square No. 1 (see Assembly Diagram), join to corresponding corner ch lp, ch 1, sc in same sp on this Square, (ch 2, join to next ch-5 lp on other Square, ch 2, skip next 2 sc on this Square, sc in next ch sp) 6 times, ch 1, join to next corner ch lp on other Square, ch 1, sc in same sp on this Square; repeat between **, join with sl st in first sc, fasten off.

Squares No. 3-59
Joining according to diagram, work same as Square No. 2.

Border
Working around entire outer edge of afghan, join off-white

with sc in corner ch sp indicated on diagram, ch 3, sc in same sp, [*ch 2, (sc, ch 3, sc) in next ch sp*; repeat between ** across to next joining, ch 2, sc in each of next 2 joined ch sps]; repeat between [ ] around to last 6 ch-5 sps; repeat between ** across to corner, ch 2, join with sl st in first sc, fasten off.✤

ASSEMBLY DIAGRAM

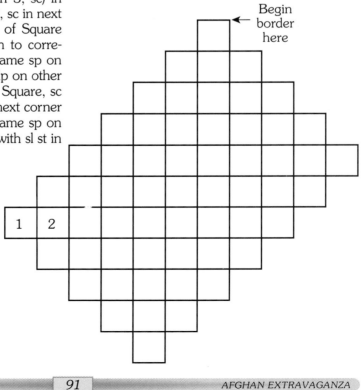

Begin border here

1 2

Zigzag Ripple

barbara roy, designer

Relax beneath these bright, bold ripples of easy single crochet. This throw will bring crisp excitement to a special room in your country home.

Finished Size
52" x 63"

Materials
Worsted-weight yarn — 24 oz. each burgundy and teal and 12 oz. white; tapestry needle; G and H crochet hooks or size needed to obtain gauge.

Gauge
G hook, 7 sc sts = 2"; 4 sc rows = 1".

Skill Level
★ Easy

Instructions

Panel (make 5 burgundy, 5 teal)

Row 1: With G hook, ch 16, 2 sc in 2nd ch from hook, sc in next 12 chs, sc last 2 chs tog, turn (15 sc).

Row 2: Ch 1, sc first 2 sts tog, sc in each st across with 2 sc in last st, turn.

Row 3: Ch 1, 2 sc in first st, sc in next 12 sts, sc last 2 sts tog, turn.

Rows 4-10: Repeat rows 2 and 3 alternately, ending with row 2.

Rows 11-20: Repeat rows 2 and 3 alternately.

Rows 21-30: Repeat rows 3 and 2 alternately.

Rows 31-240: Repeat rows 11-30 consecutively. At end of last row, fasten off.

Rnd 241: Working around outer edge of Panel, with H hook and white, join with sc in any st, sc in each st and in end of each row around with 3 sc in each corner and at each point, join with sl st in first sc, fasten off.

Alternating burgundy and teal Panels, with tapestry needle and white, sew Panels together through **back lps** *(see fig. 1, pg. 158)*.

Edging

Rnd 1: Working around entire outer edge of afghan, with H hook and white, join with sc in any st, sc in each st around with 3 sc in each corner and at each point, join with sl st in first sc.

Rnd 2: Ch 1, sc in each st around with 3 sc in each corner and at each point, join.

Rnd 3: Sl st in each st around, join with sl st in first sl st, fasten off.❧

Vintage V-Stitch

cynthia lark, designer

Subtle colors and a raised V-stitch pattern give this afghan interesting texture and timeless appeal. Worked quickly with a large hook, the design is plush as well as pretty.

Finished Size
51" x 65"

Materials
Worsted-weight yarn — 21 oz. lt. gray, 9 oz. dk. blue, 8 oz. each lt. blue, dk. rose and lt. rose; K crochet hook or size needed to obtain gauge.

Gauge
1 V-st = 1"; 2 V-st rows and 2 sc rows = 2".

Skill Level
★★ Average

Instructions
Afghan
Note: For **V-st,** (dc, ch 1, dc) in next st or ch sp.

Row 1: With dk. blue, ch 111, V-st in 5th ch from hook, skip next ch, (V-st in next ch, skip next ch) across to last ch, dc in last ch, turn, fasten off (53 V-sts).

Row 2: Join lt. gray with sc in first st, 2 sc in ch sp of next V-st; working behind sts, V-st in next skipped ch on row 1, (sc in next V-st, 3 sc in next V-st, sc in next V-st; working behind sts, V-st in next skipped ch on row 1) across to last V-st, 2 sc in last V-st, sc in last st, turn, fasten off.

Row 3: Join lt. blue with sl st in first sc, ch 3, skip next sc, V-st in next sc, skip next V-st, *(V-st in next sc, skip next sc) 2 times, V-st in next sc, skip next V-st; repeat from * across to last 3 sc, V-st in next sc, skip next sc, dc in last sc, turn, fasten off.

Row 4: Join lt. gray with sc in first st, 2 sc in next V-st; working behind sts, V-st in next skipped V-st on row before last, (sc in next V-st, 3 sc in next V-st, sc in next V-st; working behind sts, V-st in next skipped V-st on row before last) across to last V-st, 2 sc in last V-st, sc in last st, turn, fasten off.

Rows 5-128: Working in color sequence of dk. rose/lt. gray, lt. rose/lt. gray, dk. blue/lt. gray and lt. blue/lt. gray, repeat rows 3 and 4 alternately, ending with lt. rose/lt. gray.

Row 129: Join dk. blue with sl st in first sc, ch 2, hdc in each of next 2 sc, hdc in next V-st, (2 hdc in next sc, skip next sc, hdc in next sc, skip next sc, 2 hdc in next sc, hdc in next V-st) across to last 3 sc, hdc in each of last 3 sc, **do not** turn (109 hdc).

Rnd 130: Working around entire outer edge of afghan, sc in end of each row across; working on opposite side of starting ch, 3 sc in first ch, sc in each ch across with 3 sc in last ch, sc in end of each row across, 3 sc in next st, sc in each st across with 3 sc in last st, join with sl st in first sc, fasten off (484 sc).

Rnd 131: Join dk. rose with sc in any st, sc in each st around with 3 sc in each center corner st, join, fasten off (492).

Rnd 132: Join lt. gray with sl st in any center corner st, ch 6, V-st in same st, *[skip next st, (V-st in next st, skip next st) across to next center corner st], (dc, ch 3, V-st) in corner st; repeat from * 2 more times; repeat between [ ], join with sl st in 3rd ch of ch-6, fasten off.

Rnd 133: Join lt. rose with sc in any V-st, sc in same sp, 2 sc in each V-st around with sc in each center corner dc, join with sl st in first sc, fasten off.

Rnd 134: With lt. blue, repeat rnd 131.

Rnd 135: With dk. blue, repeat rnd 131. ✤

Special Gifts

Bestow a meaningful offering of affection or a simple friendly
sentiment in the form of a beautiful hand-wrought afghan
carefully chosen with the recipient in mind. Treasured
by young and old alike, they're the gift
that's always in season.

Snowy Night

shep shepherd, designer

> *Delicate snowflakes silhouetted on a bed of starry-night blue lend an ethereal quality to this lavish afghan. Its wintery look makes it excellent for holiday gift-giving.*

Finished Size
48" x 65"

Materials
Bulky yarn — 36 oz. white and 12 oz. each lt. and dk. blue; J crochet hook or size needed to obtain gauge.

Gauge
Rnd 1 of Motif = 2½" across.

Skill Level
★ Easy

Instructions

Motif No. 1

Rnd 1: With white, ch 7, sl st in first ch to form ring, ch 3, 17 dc in ring, join with sl st in top of ch-3 (18 dc).

Rnd 2: Ch 3, 2 dc in same st, ch 3, 2 dc in 3rd ch from hook, skip next 2 sts, (3 dc in next st, ch 3, 2 dc in 3rd ch from hook, skip next 2 sts) around, join.

Rnd 3: Sl st in next st, (ch 4, dc, ch 1, dc) in same st, ch 2, sc around next ch-2, ch 2, *(dc, ch 1, dc, ch 1, dc) in center st of next 3-dc group, ch 2, sc around next ch-2, ch 2; repeat from * around, join with sl st in 3rd ch of ch-4.

Note: For **V-st,** (dc, ch 2, dc) in next st.

Rnd 4: Ch 5, (*V-st in next dc, ch 2, dc in next dc, ch 2, dc in next sc, ch 2*, dc in next dc, ch 2) 5 times; repeat between **, join with sl st in 3rd ch of ch-5, fasten off.

Note: For **shell,** (2 dc, ch 2, 2 dc) in next ch sp.

Rnd 5: Join lt. blue with sl st in ch sp of any V-st, ch 3, (dc, ch 2, 2 dc) in same sp, *(ch 1, 2 dc in next ch sp) 4 times, ch 1, shell in next V-st; repeat from * 4 more times, (ch 1, 2 dc in next ch sp) 4 times, ch 1, join with sl st in top of ch-3, fasten off.

Rnd 6: Join dk. blue with sc in ch sp of any shell, ch 2, sc in same sp, *(ch 2, sc in next ch-1 sp) 5 times, ch 2, (sc, ch 2, sc) in next shell; repeat from * 4 more times, (ch 2, sc in next ch-1 sp) 5 times, ch 2, join with sl st in first sc, fasten off.

Motif No. 2

Rnds 1-5: Repeat same rnds of Motif No. 1.

Rnd 6: Join dk. blue with sc in ch sp of any shell; holding Motifs wrong sides tog, matching sts and ch sps, to **join,** ch 1, sl st in corresponding ch sp on other Motif, ch 1, sc in same shell on this Motif, (ch 1, sl st in next ch sp on other Motif, ch 1, sc in next ch-1 sp on this Motif) 5 times, ch 1, sl st in next ch sp on other Motif, ch 1, sc in next shell on this Motif, ch 1, sl st in next ch sp on other Motif, ch 1, sc in same shell on this Motif; *(ch 2, sc in next ch-1 sp) 5 times, ch 2, (sc, ch 2, sc) in next shell; repeat from * 3 more times, (ch 2, sc in next ch-1 sp) 5 times, ch 2, join with sl st in first sc, fasten off.

Motifs No. 3-31

Joining Motifs according to Assembly Diagram (pg. 108), work same as Motif No. 2.

Half Motif (make 6)

Row 1: With white, ch 7, sl st in first ch to form ring, ch 3, 9 dc in ring, turn (10 dc).

Row 2: Ch 3, 2 dc in same st, (ch 3, dc in 3rd ch from hook, skip next 2 sts, 3 dc in next

Continued on page 108

Patriotic Rickrack

roberta maier, designer

Finished Size
50" x 77"

Materials
Worsted-weight yarn — 33 oz. blue, 27 oz. red, 25 oz. white; G crochet hook or size needed to obtain gauge.

Gauge
4 sc sts = 1"; 2 dc rows = 1".

Skill Level
★ Easy

Instructions

Strip No. 1

Row 1: With white, ch 3, 3 dc in 3rd ch from hook, turn (4 dc).

Rows 2-103: Ch 2, 3 dc in first st leaving remaining sts unworked, turn. At end of last row, fasten off.

Row 104: Join blue with sc in top of ch-2 on row 1, (ch 1, 3 dc in end of next row, ch 1, sc in top of ch-2 on next row) across, turn.

Row 105: Ch 1, sc in each st and in each ch-1 sp across, fasten off.

Strip No. 2

Rows 1-103: Repeat same rows of Strip No. 1.

Row 104: With wrong side of last row facing you, join blue with sc in top of ch-2 on last row, (ch 1, 3 dc in end of next row, ch 1, sc in top of ch-2 on next row) across, turn.

Row 105: Ch 1, sc in each st and in each ch sp across, turn.

Row 106: Holding right sides of last rows on last Strip and this Strip together, matching sts, working through both thicknesses, sl st in first st, (ch 1, sl st in next st) across, fasten off.

Row 107: Working on opposite side of Strip, join red with sl st in end of row 1, ch 3, 2 dc in same row, (ch 1, sc in top of ch-2 on next row, ch 1, 3 dc in end of next row) across, turn.

Row 108: Ch 1, sc in each st and in each ch-1 sp across, fasten off.

Strip No. 3

Rows 1-103: Repeat same rows of Strip No. 1.

Row 104: With right side of last row facing you, join red with sl st in end of last row, ch 3, 2 dc in same row, (ch 1, sc in top of ch-2 on next row, ch 1, 3 dc in end of next row) across, turn.

Rows 105-106: Repeat rows 105-106 of Strip No. 2.

Row 107: Working on opposite side of Strip, join blue with sc in top of ch-2 on row 1, (ch 1, 3 dc in end of next row, ch 1, sc in top of ch-2 on next row) across, turn.

Row 108: Ch 1, sc in each st and in each ch-1 sp across, turn, fasten off.

Repeat Strips No. 2 and No. 3 ten more times.

Last Strip

Rows 1-106: Repeat same rows of Strip No. 2.✤

Winter Snowdrifts

roberta maier, designer

For those who love quiet times of peaceful escape, this breathtaking beauty will be a cherished gift. Soft and comfy, the stylish design exudes inviting hospitality and charm.

Finished Size
49" x 70" without fringe

Materials
Worsted-weight yarn — 65 oz. white; H crochet hook or size needed to obtain gauge.

Gauge
5 puff sts = 2"; 3 puff st rows and 2 sc rows = 2¼".

Skill Level
★ Easy

Instructions
Afghan
Note: For **puff st,** yo, insert hook in next ch or st, yo, draw up ½"-long lp, yo, insert hook in same ch or st, yo, draw up ½"-long lp, yo, draw through all 5 lps on hook.

Row 1: Ch 134, sc in 2nd ch from hook, sc in next 6 chs, (puff st in next 7 chs, sc in next 7 chs) across, turn (70 sc, 63 puff sts).

Row 2: Ch 1, puff st in first 7 sts, (sc in next 7 sts, puff st in next 7 sts) across, turn.

Row 3: Ch 1, sc in first 7 sts, (puff st in next 7 sts, sc in next 7 sts) across, turn.

Rows 4-159: Repeat rows 2 and 3 alternately. At end of last row, fasten off.

Fringe
For **each Fringe,** cut 3 strands each 14" long. With all three strands held together, fold in half, insert hook in st, draw fold through st, draw all loose ends through fold, tighten. Trim ends.

Fringe in each st on each short end of afghan.✣

Rubies & Diamonds

roberta maier, designer

Medallions and diamonds combine to create this graceful throw that will be a welcome addition to anyone's home. Lacy trim adds a romantic note to the traditional styling.

Finished Size
51" x 74"

Materials
Worsted-weight yarn — 60 oz. off-white; size 10 bedspread cotton — 400 yds. red; sewing needle; red sewing thread; No. 6 steel and G crochet hooks or sizes needed to obtain gauges.

Gauges
G hook and worsted-weight,
4 sc sts = 1"; 4 sc rows = 1".
No. 6 steel hook and bedspread cotton,
Medallion is 2½" across.

Skill Level
★★ Average

Instructions

Medallion (make 45)
Rnd 1: With No. 6 hook and red, ch 4, sl st in first ch to form ring, ch 1, 8 sc in ring, join with sl st in first sc (8 sc).

Rnd 2: Ch 1, sc in first st, (ch 4, sc in next st) around, ch 2, join with dc in first st (8 ch sps).

Rnd 3: Ch 3, 2 dc around joining dc, 3 dc in each ch sp around, join with sl st in top of ch-3 (24 dc).

Rnd 4: Ch 3, dc in same st, dc in next st, 2 dc in next st, ch 1, (2 dc in next st, dc in next st, 2 dc in next st, ch 1) around, join (40 dc, 8 ch-1 sps).

Rnd 5: (*Ch 3, tr in same st, dc in next st, hdc in next st, dc in next st, tr in next st, ch 3, sl st in same st as last tr, sc in next ch-1 sp*, sl st in next st) 7 times; repeat between **, join with sl st in joining sl st of last rnd, fasten off.

Panel No. 1 (make 4)
Row 1: With G hook and off-white, ch 26, sc in 2nd ch from hook, sc in each ch across, turn (25 sc).

Note: For **puff stitch (ps),** yo, insert hook in next st, yo, draw up long lp, (yo, insert hook in same st, yo, draw up long lp) 2 times, yo, draw through all 7 lps on hook.

Row 2: Ch 1, sc in first 12 sts, ps, sc in last 12 sts, turn.

Row 3: Ch 1, sc in each st across, turn.

Row 4: Ch 1, sc in first 10 sts, ps, sc in each of next 3 sts, ps, sc in last 10 sts, turn.

Row 5: Ch 1, sc in each st across, turn.

Row 6: Ch 1, sc in first 8 sts, ps, sc in next 7 sts, ps, sc in last 8 sts, turn.

Row 7: Ch 1, sc in each st across, turn.

Row 8: Ch 1, sc in first 6 sts, ps, sc in next 11 sts, ps, sc in last 6 sts, turn.

Row 9: Ch 1, sc in each st across, turn.

Row 10: Ch 1, sc in first 4 sts, ps, (sc in next 7 sts, ps) 2 times, sc in last 4 sts, turn.

Row 11: Ch 1, sc in each st across, turn.

Row 12: Ch 1, sc in each of first 2 sts, ps, sc in next 7 sts, ps, sc in each of next 3 sts, ps, sc in next 7 sts, ps, sc in each of last 2 sts, turn.

Row 13: Ch 1, sc in each st across, turn.

Rows 14-22: Working in reverse order, repeat rows 10-2.

Row 23: Ch 1, sc in each st across, turn.

Rows 24-31: Repeat rows 2-9.

Row 32: Ch 1, sc in first 4 sts, ps, sc in next 15 sts, ps, sc in last 4 sts, turn.

Continued on page 109

Winter Roses

elizabeth a. white, designer

Give a lasting bouquet they can treasure forever! A delightful medley of dark red roses on a soft white background sets this afghan apart as something special.

Finished Size
49½" x 66½"

Materials
Worsted-weight yarn — 57 oz. burgundy, 29 oz. ecru and 15 oz. green; J crochet hook or size needed to obtain gauge.

Gauge
5 dc sts = 2"; 5 dc rows = 3".
Each Block is 8½" square.

Skill Level
★ Easy

Instructions
Block (make 35)

Note: For **reverse shell,** (yo, insert hook in next st, yo, draw lp through, yo, draw through 2 lps on hook) 3 times, yo, draw through all 4 lps on hook.

Rnd 1: With burgundy, ch 6, sl st in first ch to form ring, ch 3, 3 dc in ring, **turn,** ch 2, reverse shell, **turn,** ch 5, (4 dc in ring, **turn,** ch 2, reverse shell, **turn,** ch 5) 7 times, join with sl st in top of ch-3, fasten off (8 reverse shells).

Note: For **beginning treble cluster (beg tr cl),** ch 4, *yo 2 times, insert hook in same ch sp, yo, draw lp through, (yo, draw through 2 lps on hook) 2 times; repeat from *, yo, draw through all 3 lps on hook.

For **treble cluster (tr cl),** yo 2 times, insert hook in next ch sp, yo, draw lp through, (yo, draw through 2 lps on hook) 2 times, *yo 2 times, insert hook in same ch sp, yo, draw lp through, (yo, draw through 2 lps on hook) 2 times; repeat from *, yo, draw through all 4 lps on hook.

Rnd 2: Join green with sl st in any ch-5 sp, beg tr cl, ch 3, (tr cl, ch 3, tr cl) in next ch sp, ch 3, *tr cl in next ch sp, ch 3, (tr cl, ch 3, tr cl) in next ch sp, ch 3; repeat from * around, join with sl st in top of first cl, fasten off.

Rnd 3: Join ecru with sl st in ch-3 sp between any 2-cl group, (ch 3, 2 dc, ch 3, 3 dc) in same sp, ch 1, (3 dc, ch 1) in each of next 2 ch sps, *(3 dc, ch 3, 3 dc) in next ch sp, ch 1, (3 dc, ch 1) in each of next 2 ch sps; repeat from * 2 more times, join with sl st in top of ch-3.

Rnd 4: Sl st in each of next 2 sts, sl st in next ch sp, (ch 3, 2 dc, ch 3, 3 dc) in same sp, ch 1, (3 dc, ch 1) in each of next 3 ch sps, *(3 dc, ch 3, 3 dc) in next ch sp, ch 1, (3 dc, ch 1) in each of next 3 ch sps; repeat from * 2 more times, join, fasten off.

Rnd 5: Join burgundy with sl st in any st, ch 3, dc in each st and in each ch-1 sp around with (3 dc, ch 1, 3 dc) in each corner ch-3 sp, join, fasten off.

To **join,** hold Blocks right sides together, matching sts; working in **back lps** *(see fig. 1, pg. 158)* through both thicknesses, join burgundy with sl st in any ch-1 sp, sl st in each st across to next ch-1 sp, fasten off.

Join Blocks in five strips of seven Blocks each.

Border

Rnd 1: Working around entire outer edge, join burgundy with sl st in any st, ch 3, dc in each st around with (dc, ch 1, dc) in each corner ch-1 sp, join with sl st in top of ch-3, **turn.**

Rnds 2-5: Ch 3, dc in each st around with (dc, ch 1, dc) in each corner ch-1 sp, **turn.** At end of last rnd, **do not** turn.

Rnd 6: Ch 1, reverse sc *(see fig.10, pg. 159)* in each st and in each ch sp around, join with sl st in first sc, fasten off.✤

Snowy Night

Continued from page 98

st) across, turn.

Row 3: Ch 4, dc in next st, ch 1, dc in next st, *ch 2, sc around next ch-2, ch 2, (dc, ch 1, dc, ch 1, dc) in center dc of next 3-dc group; repeat from * 1 more time, ch 2, sc around next ch-2, ch 2, dc in next dc, (ch 1, dc in next dc) 2 times, turn.

Row 4: Ch 5, dc in next dc, (*ch 2, dc in next dc, ch 2, dc in next sc, ch 2, dc in next dc, ch 2*, V-st in next dc) 2 times; repeat between **, dc in next dc, ch 2, dc in last dc, turn, fasten off.

Row 5: Join lt. blue with sl st in first ch sp, ch 3, dc in same sp, *ch 1, (2 dc in next ch sp, ch 1) across to next V-st, shell in next V-st; repeat from * 1 more time, (ch 1, 2 dc in next ch sp) across, **do not** turn, fasten off.

Rnd 6: Join dk. blue with sc in space between first and 2nd sts, ch 1, sl st in corresponding ch sp on other Motif (see Assembly Diagram), ch 1, sc in same sp on this Motif, *[(ch 1, sl st in next ch sp on other Motif, ch 1, sc in next ch-1 sp on this Motif) 5 times, ch 1, sl st in next ch sp on other Motif, ch 1], sc in next shell on this Motif, ch 1, sl st in next ch sp on other Motif, ch 1, sc in same shell on this Motif; repeat from * 1 more time; repeat between [ ], sc in sp between last 2 sts on this Motif, ch 1, sc in next ch sp on other Motif, ch 1, sc in same sp on this Motif; working in ends of rows, (ch 2, sc in end of next row) 4 times, ch 2, sc in beginning ring, (ch 2, sc in end of next row) 5 times, ch 2, join with sl st in first sc, fasten off.

Border

Join white with sl st in ch sp at top right corner as indicated on Assembly Diagram; for **tassel,** ch 23, 3 dc in 3rd ch from hook, drop lp from hook, insert hook in first dc, pick up dropped lp, draw through st, ch 3, sl st in same ch as last dc, ch 19; sl st in same ch sp as first sl st, (sl st, tassel, sl st) in each ch sp across to top left corner, ch 3, (sl st in next ch sp, ch 3) across to bottom left corner, (sl st, tassel, sl st) in each ch sp across to bottom right corner, ch 3, (sl st in next ch sp, ch 3) across, join with sl st in first sl st, fasten off.✿

Assembly Diagram

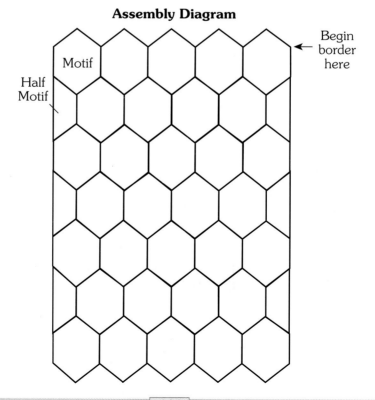

Rubies & Diamonds

Continued from page 105

Row 33: Ch 1, sc in each st across, turn.

Row 34: Ch 1, sc in each of first 2 sts, ps, sc in next 19 sts, ps, sc in each of last 2 sts, turn.

Row 35: Ch 1, sc in each st across, turn.

Rows 36-37: Repeat rows 32 and 33.

Rows 38-44: Repeat rows 8-2.

Row 45: Ch 1, sc in each st across, turn.

Rows 46-287: Repeat rows 2-45 consecutively, ending with row 23. At end of last row, **do not** turn.

Row 288: Ch 1, sc in end of each row across, fasten off.

Row 289: Working on opposite side of Panel, join with sc in end of row 1, sc in end of each row across, fasten off.

Panel No. 2 (make 3)

Row 1: With G hook and off-white, ch 26, sc in 2nd ch from hook, sc in each ch across, turn (25 sc).

Row 2: Ch 1, sc in first 12 sts, ps, sc in last 12 sts, turn.

Row 3: Ch 1, sc in each st across, turn.

Row 4: Ch 1, sc in first 10 sts, ps, sc in each of next 3 sts, ps, sc in last 10 sts, turn.

Row 5: Ch 1, sc in each st across, turn.

Row 6: Ch 1, sc in first 8 sts, ps, sc in next 7 sts, ps, sc in last 8 sts, turn.

Row 7: Ch 1, sc in each st across, turn.

Row 8: Ch 1, sc in first 6 sts, ps, sc in next 11 sts, ps, sc in last 6 sts, turn.

Row 9: Ch 1, sc in each st across, turn.

Row 10: Ch 1, sc in first 4 sts, ps, sc in next 15 sts, ps, sc in last 4 sts, turn.

Row 11: Ch 1, sc in each st across, turn.

Row 12: Ch 1, sc in each of first 2 sts, ps, sc in next 19 sts, ps, sc in each of last 2 sts, turn.

Row 13: Ch 1, sc in each st across, turn.

Rows 14-22: Repeat rows 10-2.

Row 23: Ch 1, sc in each st across, turn.

Rows 24-31: Repeat rows 2-9.

Row 32: Ch 1, sc in first 4 sts, ps, (sc in next 7 sts, ps) 2 times, sc in last 4 sts, turn.

Row 33: Ch 1, sc in each st across, turn.

Row 34: Ch 1, sc in each of first 2 sts, ps, sc in next 7 sts, ps, sc in each of next 3 sts, ps, sc in next 7 sts, ps, sc in each of last 2 sts, turn.

Row 35: Ch 1, sc in each st across, turn.

Rows 36-37: Repeat rows 32 and 33.

Rows 38-44: Repeat rows 8-2.

Row 45: Ch 1, sc in each st across, turn.

Rows 46-287: Repeat rows 2-45 consecutively, ending with row 23. At end of last row, **do not** turn.

Rows 288-289: Repeat same rows of Panel No. 1.

Assembly

To **join Panels,** hold one of each Panel wrong sides together with Panel No. 1 facing you; working through both thicknesses, with G hook, join off-white with sl st in first st on long edge, (ch 1, sl st in next st) across, fasten off.

Alternating Panels and beginning each joining at same end, repeat with remaining Panels.

Border

Rnd 1: Working around entire outer edge, with G hook and off-white, join with sc in corner st on one short end, 2 sc in same st, sc in each st, in end of each row and in each seam around with 3 sc in each corner, join with sl st in first sc (972 sc).

Rnd 2: Ch 1, sc in each st around with 3 sc in each center corner st, join (980).

Rnd 3: Sl st to next center corner st, ch 1, (sc, ch 7, sc) in same st, ch 5, skip next 2 sts, *(sc in next st, ch 5, skip next 2 sts) across to next center corner st, (sc, ch 7, sc) in next corner st*, ch 5, skip next 3 sts; repeat between **, ch 5, skip next 2 sts; repeat between **, ch 5, skip next 3 sts, (sc in next st, ch 5, skip next 2 sts) across to next corner, join.

Rnd 4: Ch 1, *(sc, hdc, dc, tr, dc, hdc, sc) in next ch-7 sp, sc in next ch-5 sp, (ch 5, sc in next ch-5 sp) across to next corner ch-7 sp; repeat from * around, join, fasten off.

With sewing needle and thread, sew one Medallion to center of each diamond without center puff stitches.✤

Contemporary Chic

Sleek artistic lines coupled with bold graphic colors catch your eye with instant, lasting appeal. Spread your wings and freely indulge in the unbridled fulfillment of all your crochet fantasies with these superb examples of modern needlecraft.

Enchantment

roberta maier, designer

Bask in the rosy glow of elegance with this quickly made mile-a-minute. Delicate strips of pink bordered in rich black lend charm to this splendid design.

Finished Size
48" x 75"

Materials
Worsted-weight yarn — 43 oz. pink and 29 oz. black; G crochet hook or size needed to obtain gauge.

Gauge
3 dc sts = ¾"; 1 dc row = ¾".

Skill Level
★ Easy

Instructions

Strip (make 12)

Row 1: With pink, ch 14, sc in 2nd ch from hook, (ch 3, skip next 3 chs, sc in next ch) across, turn (4 sc, 3 ch sps).

Row 2: Ch 3, 3 dc in each of next 3 ch sps, dc in last sc, turn (11 dc). Front of row 2 is right side of work.

Row 3: Ch 1, sc in first st, (ch 3, sc in space between next two 3-dc groups) 2 times, ch 3, sc in last st, turn.

Rows 4-165: Repeat rows 2 and 3 alternately. At end of last row, fasten off.

Note: For **double treble crochet (dtr)** *(see fig. 8, pg. 159),* yo 3 times, insert hook in next st, yo, draw lp through, (yo, draw through 2 lps on hook) 4 times.

Rnd 166: Working in ends of rows around outer edge, join black with sl st in end of row 2, ch 3, 2 dc in same row, 3 dc in end of each dc row across, skip next ch-3 sp, 15 dtr in next ch-3 sp, 3 dc in end of each dc row across, skip next ch-3 sp, 15 dtr in next ch-3 sp, join with sl st in top of ch-3, fasten off.

Assembly

Holding two Strips wrong sides together, matching sts, working through both thicknesses, join black with sl st in first dc on one edge, (ch 1, sl st in next dc) across leaving dtrs at ends unworked, fasten off.

Repeat with remaining Strips.

Border

Working around entire outer edge, with right side facing you, join black with sc in first dtr on one end, sc in next 7 sts; for **picot,** ch 3, sl st in last st made; *(sc in next 15 dtr, picot) 11 times, sc in last 7 dtr, sc in each dc across*, sc in next 8 dtr, picot; repeat between **, join with sl st in first sc, fasten off.❧

Celestial Lights

katherine eng, designer

Launch the decor of your secret hideaway into orbit! Bright suns, twinkling stars and golden moons arrayed on midnight blue adorn this heavenly afghan.

Finished Size
45" x 60"

Materials
Worsted-weight yarn — 46 oz. blue and 12½ oz. gold; tapestry needle; F crochet hook or size needed to obtain gauge.

Gauge
Each Square is 5" x 5".

Skill Level
★★ Average

Instructions

Sun Square (make 24)

Rnd 1: With gold, ch 4, sl st in first ch to form ring, ch 1, 8 sc in ring, join with sl st in first sc (8 sc).

Rnd 2: Ch 1, sc in first st, 2 sc in next st, (sc in next st, 2 sc in next st) around, join (12).

Rnd 3: Ch 1, sc in first st, ch 7, sc in next st, ch 9, (sc in next st, ch 7, sc in next st, ch 9) around, join, fasten off (6 ch-7 lps, 6 ch-9 lps).

Rnd 4: Join blue with sc in 5th ch of any ch-9, *[ch 1, dc in **back lp** *(see fig. 1, pg. 158)* of next sc, ch 1, hdc in 4th ch of next ch-7, ch 1,

dc in **back lp** of next sc, ch 1], sc in 5th ch of next ch-9; repeat from * 4 more times; repeat between [ ], join (12 dc, 6 sc, 6 hdc).

Rnd 5: Ch 1, sc in each st and in each ch-1 sp around, join (48 sc).

Rnd 6: Ch 1, sc in each of first 3 sts, *[hdc in each of next 2 sts, dc in next st, (2 dc, ch 3, 2 dc) in next st, dc in next st, hdc in each of next 2 sts], sc in next 5 sts; repeat from * 2 more times; repeat between [ ], sc in each of last 2 sts, join.

Rnd 7: Ch 1, sc in each st around with (sc, ch 3, sc) in each corner ch sp, join, fasten off (17 sc on each side between ch-3 sps).

Star Square (make 23)

Rnd 1: With gold, ch 4, sl st in first ch to form ring, ch 1, (sc in ring, ch 3) 4 times, sc in ring, ch 1, join with hdc in first sc (5 sc, 5 ch sps).

Rnd 2: Ch 1, (sc, ch 3, sc) around joining hdc, *ch 1, (sc, ch 3, sc) in next ch sp; repeat from * around, ch 1, join with sl st in first sc.

Rnd 3: Ch 1, sc in first st, *[(2 sc, ch 3, 2 sc) in next ch sp, sc in next sc, sl st in next ch-1 sp], sc in next sc; repeat from * 3 more times; repeat between [ ], join.

Rnd 4: Ch 2, skip next st, sl st in next st, *[ch 2, (sl st, ch 3, sl st) in next ch-3 sp, ch 2, sl st in next sc, ch 2, skip next 2 sts], sl st in next sl st, ch 2, skip next 2 sts, sl st in next sc; repeat from * 3 times; repeat between [ ], join with sl st in joining sl st of last rnd, fasten off (20 ch-2 sps, 5 ch-3 sps).

Rnd 5: Join blue with sc in any ch-3 sp, sc in same sp, *[2 dc in next ch-2 sp, 2 tr in each of next 2 ch-2 sps, 2 dc in next ch-2 sp], 2 sc in next ch-3 sp; repeat from * 3 more times; repeat between [ ], join with sl st in first sc (50 sts).

Rnd 6: Ch 1, skip first st, sc in each of next 3 sts, *[hdc in each of next 2 sts, dc in next st, (2 dc, ch 3, 2 dc) in next st, dc in next st, hdc in each of next 2 sts], sc in next 5 sts*; repeat between **, skip next st; repeat between **; repeat between [ ], sc in each of last 2 sts, join.

Continued on page 116

Celestial Lights

Continued from page 115

Rnd 7: Ch 1, sc in each st around with (sc, ch 3, sc) in each corner ch sp, join, fasten off (17 sc on each side between ch-3 sps).

Moon Square (make 23)

Rnd 1: With blue, ch 6, sc in 2nd ch from hook, sc in each of next 3 chs, (sc, ch 2, sc) in last ch; working on opposite side of ch, sc in next 3 chs, (sc, ch 2) in last ch, join with sl st in first sc (10 sc, 2 ch sps).

Rnd 2: Ch 1, sc in each of first 2 sts, *2 sc in next st, sc in each of next 2 sts, (sc, ch 2, sc) in next ch sp*, sc in each of next 2 sts; repeat between **, join.

Rnd 3: Ch 1, sc in each of first 2 sts, *2 sc in each of next 2 sts, sc in each of next 3 sts, (sc, ch 2, sc) in next ch sp*, sc in each of next 3 sts; repeat between **, sc in last st, join, fasten off.

Row 4: Working in rows, join gold with sc in first ch-2 sp, sc in each of next 2 sts, hdc in each of next 2 sts, 2 dc in next st, dc in each of next 2 sts, 2 dc in next st, hdc in each of next 2 sts, sc in each of next 2 sts, sc in next ch-2 sp leaving remaining sts unworked, turn (16 sts).

Note: Sl sts are not used or counted as sts.

Row 5: Sl st in first st, ch 1, sc next 2 sts tog, 2 hdc in next st, sc in each of next 3 sts, 2 sc in each of next 2 sts, sc in next 4 sts, sc next 2 sts tog leaving last st unworked, turn (15 sts).

Row 6: Sl st in first st, ch 1, sc next 2 sts tog, (ch 1, sc in next st) 10 times, sc last 2 sts tog, **do not** turn.

Rnd 7: Ch 3, sl st in end of row 4, ch 3, skip next st on rnd 3, sl st in next st, ch 3, sl st in next st, (ch 3, skip next st, sl st in next st) 4 times, ch 3, skip next st, sl st in ch-2 sp on rnd 3, ch 3, sl st in 2nd sc on row 4 (mark last ch sp made), ch 3, sl st in end of row 5, ch 3, skip next st, sl st in next ch-1 sp, (ch 3, skip next st, next ch-1 sp and next st, sc in next ch-1 sp) 5 times, join with sl st in first ch of first ch-3, fasten off (16 ch sps).

Rnd 8: Join blue with sc in marked ch sp, sc in same sp, 3 sc in each ch sp around, sc in same ch sp as first sc, join with sl st in first sc (48 sc).

Rnd 9: Ch 1, sc in each of first 3 sts, *[hdc in each of next 2 sts, dc in next st, (2 dc, ch 3, 2 dc) in next st, dc in next st, hdc in each of next 2 sts], sc in next 5 sts; repeat from * 2 more times; repeat between [ ], sc in each of last 2 sts, join.

Rnd 10: Ch 1, sc in each st around with (sc, ch 3, sc) in each corner ch sp, join, fasten off (17 sc on each side between ch-3 sps).

With tapestry needle and blue, working in **back lps** only, sew Squares together in seven rows of ten blocks each according to Assembly Diagram.

Border

Rnd 1: Join blue with sc in any st on one long edge, sc in each st, hdc in each ch sp on each side of seams, and hdc in each seam around with (sc, ch 3, sc) in each corner ch sp, join with sl st in first sc (139 sts on each short end, 199 sts on each long edge, 4 ch sps).

Rnd 2: Ch 1, sc in each st around with (sc, ch 3, sc) in each corner ch sp, join, fasten off.

Rnd 3: Join gold with sl st in any corner ch sp, ch 3, sl st in same sp, *[ch 2, skip next st, (sl st in next st, ch 2, skip next st) across to next corner], (sl st, ch 3, sl st) in corner ch sp; repeat from * 2 more times; repeat between [ ], join with sl st in first sl st, fasten off.

Rnd 4: Join blue with sc in any ch-2 sp, ch 1, (sc, ch 1) in each ch-2 sp around with (sc, ch 3, sc, ch 1) in each corner ch-3 sp, join with sl st in first sc, **turn.**

Rnd 5: Ch 1, sc in first ch-1 sp, ch 1, (sc, ch 1) in each ch-1 sp around with (sc, ch 3, sc, ch 1) in each corner ch-3 sp, join, **turn.**

Rnd 6: Ch 1, sc in each st and in each ch sp around with (sc, ch 3, sc) in each corner ch-3 sp, join, **do not** turn, fasten off.

Rnd 7: Repeat rnd 3, **do not** fasten off.

Rnd 8: Sl st in first corner ch sp, ch 1, (sc, ch 3, sc) in same sp, ch 1, (sc, ch 1) in each ch-2 sp around with (sc, ch 3, sc, ch 1) in each corner ch-3 sp, join, **turn.**

Rnd 9: Repeat rnd 5, fasten off.

Rnd 10: Join blue with sc in first ch sp after any corner ch sp, ch 1, (sc, ch 1) in each ch sp around with (sc, ch 3, sc, ch 1) in each corner ch-3 sp, join.

Rnd 11: Sl st in next ch sp, ch 2, (sl st, ch 2) in each ch sp around with (sl st, ch 3, sl st, ch 2) in each corner ch-3 sp, join with sl st in first sl st.

Rnd 12: Sl st in next ch sp, ch 1, sc in

same sp, [*(sc, ch 3, sc) in next ch sp, sc in next ch sp; repeat from * across to next corner, (sc, ch 3, sc, ch 3, sc, ch 3, sc) in next corner ch-3 sp, sc in next ch sp]; repeat between [ ] 3 times, (sc, ch 3, sc) in last ch sp, join with sl st in first sc.

Note: For **shell,** (2 dc, ch 2, 2 dc) in next ch sp.

Rnd 13: Sl st in next st, (sl st, ch 3, dc, ch 2, 2 dc) in next ch-3 sp, shell in each ch-3 sp around, join with sl st in top of ch-3.

Rnd 14: Sl st in next st, sl st in next ch sp, ch 1, (sc, ch 3, sc, ch 3) in same sp, (sc, ch 3, sc, ch 3) in ch sp of each shell around, join with sl st in first sc.

Rnd 15: Sl st in next ch sp, ch 3, (dc, ch 2, 2 dc) in same sp, sc in next ch sp, (shell in next ch sp, sc in next ch sp) around, join with sl st in top of ch-3.

Rnd 16: Sl st in next st, sl st in next ch-2 sp, ch 1, (sc, ch 3, sc) in same sp, ch 1, sc in next sc, ch 1, [*(sc, ch 3, sc) in next shell, ch 1, sc in next sc, ch 1; repeat from * across to next 3 corner shells, ch 2, (sc, ch 3, sc) in next shell, ch 2, sc in next sc, ch 2, (sc, ch 3, sc, ch 5, sc, ch 3, sc) in next shell, ch 2, sc in next sc, ch 2, (sc, ch 3, sc) in next shell, ch 2, sc in next sc]; repeat between [ ] 3 more times, ch 1, (sc, ch 3, sc) in next shell, ch 1, sc in next sc, ch 1, join with sl st in first sc.

Rnd 17: Sl st in first ch-3 sp, (ch 3, sl st) in same sp, ch 2, sl st in next sc, [*◊ch 2, (sl st, ch 3, sl st) in next ch-3 sp, ch 2, sl st in next sc◊; repeat from * across to next 3 center corner ch sps, ch 3, sl st in same sc, ch 2, (sl st, ch 3, sl st) in next ch-3 sp, ch 2, (sl st, ch 3, sl st) in next ch-5 sp, ch 2, (sl st, ch 3, sl st) in next ch-3 sp, ch 2, (sl st, ch 3, sl st) in next sc]; repeat between [ ] 3 more times; repeat between ◊◊ 2 more times, ch 2, join, fasten off.✤

ASSEMBLY DIAGRAM

◯ = Sun Square

☾ = Moon Square

☆ = Star Square

Holiday Squares & Stripes

katherine eng, designer

Sleek geometric lines created by a tranquil blend of teal and rich jeweltones make this lovely afghan a designer essential. It's a super conversation piece!

Finished Size
48" x 65½"

Materials
Worsted-weight yarn — 24 oz. teal, 16 oz. navy, 11 oz. dk. red, 4½ oz. med. blue, 2½ oz. each coral, lt. purple, dk. purple and lt. blue; I crochet hook or size needed to obtain gauge.

Gauge
3 sc sts = 1"; 3 sc rows = 1".

Skill Level
★★ Average

Instructions
Strip No. 1

Row 1: With teal, ch 12, sc in 2nd ch from hook, sc in each ch across, turn (11 sc). Front of row 1 is right side of work.

Row 2: Ch 1, sc in first st, (ch 1, skip next st, sc in next st) across, turn.

Row 3: Ch 1, sc in each st and in each ch sp across, turn.

Rows 4-10: Repeat rows 2 and 3 alternately, ending with row 2. At end of last row, fasten off.

Row 11: Join med. blue with sc in first st, sc in each ch sp and in each st across, turn.

Rows 12-20: Repeat rows 2-10.

Rows 21-170: Working in color sequence of teal, coral, teal, lt. purple, teal, dk. red, teal, lt. blue, teal, dk. purple, teal, lt. purple, teal, coral, teal, repeat rows 11-20 consecutively.

Row 171: For **edging,** with right side facing you, join navy with sc in starting ch on lower right-hand corner, sc in end of each row across, turn (171 sc).

Row 172: Ch 1, sc in first st, (ch 1, skip next st, sc in next st) across, turn.

Row 173: Ch 1, sc in each st and in each ch sp across, turn, fasten off.

Row 174: Join teal with sl st in first st, ch 2, dc in same st, *skip next st, (sl st, ch 2, dc) in next st; repeat from * across to last 2 sts, skip next st, sl st in last st, turn.

Row 175: Ch 4, sc in next ch-2 sp, (ch 1, sc in next ch-2 sp) across, turn, fasten off (85 ch sps).

Row 176: Join dk. red with sc in first ch sp, ch 2, sc in same sp, (sc, ch 2, sc) in each ch sp across, turn, fasten off.

Row 177: With navy, repeat row 176.

Row 178: Working on opposite side of Strip, join navy with sc in end of last row, sc in end of each row across, sc in first ch on opposite side of starting ch, turn (171 sc).

Rows 179-183: Repeat rows 172-176.

Strip No. 2

Rows 1-170: Working in color sequence of lt. purple, teal, dk. red, teal, lt. blue, teal, dk. purple, teal, med. blue, teal, coral, teal, dk. red, teal, lt. blue, teal, med. blue, repeat same rows of Strip No. 1.

Continued on page 127

Contemporary Diamonds

rena v. stevens, designer

Diamonds may be a girl's best friend, but the man in your life will also find himself drawn to this stylish design. It's extra large and snuggly with tassels that add a special flair.

Finished Size
66" x 88½" without tassles

Materials
Worsted-weight yarn — 55 oz. heather gray and 34 oz. black; tapestry needle; J crochet hook or size needed to obtain gauge.

Gauge
3 dc sts = 1"; each Diamond is 13" x 17½".

Skill Level
★★★ Challenging

Instructions

Diamond No. 1 (make 22)

Rnd 1: With black, ch 5, sl st in first ch to form ring, ch 1, 12 sc in ring, join with sl st in first sc (12 sc).

Rnd 2: Working this rnd in **back lps** only *(see fig.1, pg. 158)*, ch 1, sc in first 5 sts, (2 sc, ch 1, 2 sc) in next st, sc in next 5 sts, (2 sc, ch 1, 2 sc) in last st, join, fasten off.

Rnd 3: Join gray with sc in **back lp** of any ch-1; for **end ch sp,** ch 1; sc in same ch, *(sc in next st, sc in **back lp** of next st) 2 times, (sc, ch 1, sc) in next st, (sc in **back lp** of next st, sc in next st) 2 times*, (sc; for **end ch sp,** ch 1; sc) in **back lp** of next ch-1; repeat between **, join, fasten off (24 sc, 4 ch sps).

Rnd 4: Join black with sc in any end ch-1 sp, ch 1, sc in same sp, sc in next 6 sts, sc in next ch sp, sc in next 6 sts, (sc, ch 1, sc) in next ch sp, sc in next 6 sts, sc in next ch sp, sc in last 6 sts, join, fasten off (30 sc, 2 ch sps).

Note: For **long single crochet (lsc),** working over sts, insert hook in next st on rnd before last, draw up long lp same height as last st on rnd being worked, yo, draw through both lps on hook.

Rnd 5: Join gray with sc in any ch-1 sp; for **end ch sp,** ch 1; sc in same sp, *(sc in **back lp** of next st, lsc) 3 times, sc in **back lp** of next st, (lsc, ch 1, lsc) in next ch-1 sp on rnd before last, (sc in **back lp** of next st, lsc) 3 times, sc in **back lp** of next st*, (sc; for **end ch sp,** ch 1; sc) in next ch sp; repeat between **, join, fasten off.

Rnd 6: Join black with sl st in any end ch sp, ch 3, (dc, ch 3, 2 dc) in same sp, *dc in next 9 sts, (dc, ch 1, dc) in next ch-1 sp, dc in next 9 sts*, (2 dc, ch 3, 2 dc) in next ch sp; repeat between **, join with sl st in top of ch-3, **do not** fasten off.

Rnd 7: Sl st in next st, ch 1, sc in same st, *ch 1, (sc, hdc, ch 1, hdc, sc) in next end ch sp, (ch 1, skip next st, sc in next st) 6 times, ch 1, (hdc, ch 2, hdc) in next ch sp*, (ch 1, skip next st, sc in next st) 6 times; repeat between **, (ch 1, skip next st, sc in next st) 5 times, ch 1, join, fasten off.

Note: For **long double crochet (ldc),** working over sts, yo, insert hook in next st or ch sp on rnd before last, draw up long lp same height as last st on rnd being worked, (yo, draw through 2 lps on hook) 2 times.

Continued on page 122

Contemporary Diamonds

Continued from page 120

Rnd 8: Join gray with sl st in any end ch-1 sp, ch 4, hdc in same sp, *sc in next hdc, sc in next sc, ldc in end ch-3 sp on rnd before last, (sc in next st, ldc) 5 times, sc in next st, ldc in next ch sp on rnd before last, skip next hdc, (sc, ch 1, sc) in next ch-2 sp, skip next hdc, ldc in same ch-1 sp on rnd before last as last ldc, (sc in next sc, ldc) 5 times, sc in next st, ldc in end ch-3 sp on rnd before last, sc in next sc, sc in next hdc*, (hdc, ch 2, hdc) in next end ch sp; repeat between **, join with sl st in 2nd ch of ch-4, fasten off.

Rnd 9: Join black with sc in any end ch-2 sp, ch 1, sc in same sp, ch 1, *sc in next hdc, ch 1, skip next sc, (sc in next sc, ch 1, skip next ldc) 7 times, sc in next sc, ch 1, sc in next ch-1 sp, ch 1, (sc in next sc, ch 1, skip next ldc) 7 times, sc in next sc, ch 1, skip next sc, sc in next hdc, ch 1*, (sc, ch 1, sc) in next end ch sp; repeat between **, join, fasten off.

Rnd 10: Join gray with sl st in any end ch sp, ch 6, dc in same sp, *skip next st, hdc in next ch sp, (sc in **back lp** of next st, ldc) 8 times, sc in **back lp** of next st, sc in next ch sp, ch 1, sc in **back lp** of next st, ch 1, sc in next ch sp, (sc in **back lp** of next st, ldc) 8 times, sc in **back lp** of next st, hdc in next ch sp, skip next st*, (dc, ch 3, dc) in next end ch sp; repeat between **, join with sl st in 3rd ch

ASSEMBLY DIAGRAM

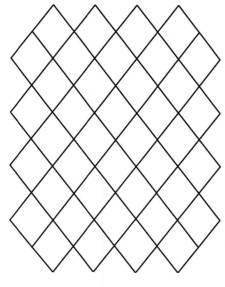

of ch-6, fasten off.

Note: For **cluster (cl),** yo, insert hook in next st or ch sp, yo, draw lp through, yo, draw through 2 lps on hook, yo, insert hook in same st or ch sp, yo, draw lp through, yo, draw through 2 lps on hook, yo, draw through all 3 lps on hook.

Rnd 11: Join black with sl st in hdc before any end ch sp, ch 3, dc in same st, *(cl, dc, ch 3, dc, cl) in next ch sp, (skip next st, cl in next st) 10 times, skip next ch sp, (dc, ch 3, dc) in next sc, skip next ch sp,* (cl in next st, skip next st) 10 times; repeat between **, (cl in next st, skip next st) 9 times, join with sl st in top of first dc, fasten off. (First ch-3 and dc count as one cl).

Rnd 12: Join gray with sc in any end ch sp, (sc, ch 2, 2 sc) in same sp; *working in spaces between cls and dc, 2 sc in each of next 12 sps, (sc, ch 1, sc) in next ch-3 sp, 2 sc in each of next 12 sps*, (2 sc, ch 2, 2 sc) in next end ch sp; repeat between **, join, fasten off.

Rnd 13: Join black with sl st in any end ch sp, ch 4, (tr, ch 2, 2 tr) in same sp, *skip next 2 sts, 2 dc in next st, (skip next st, 2 dc in next st) 12 times, (dc, ch 2, dc) in next ch-1 sp, (skip next st, 2 dc in next st) 13 times*, (2 tr, ch 2, 2 tr) in next end ch sp; repeat between **, join with sl st in top of ch-4, fasten off.

Rnd 14: Join gray with sl st in any end ch sp, ch 5, hdc in same sp, *ch 2, sc in sp between next 2 tr, (ch 1, sc in sp between next 2 dc) 13 times, ch 1, skip next st, (hdc, ch 2, hdc) in next ch sp, skip next st, (ch 1, sc in sp between next 2 dc) 13 times, ch 1, sc in sp between next 2 tr, ch 2*, (hdc, ch 3, hdc) in next end ch sp; repeat between **, join with sl st in 2nd ch of ch-5, **do not** fasten off.

Rnd 15: Sl st in next ch sp, ch 1, (2 sc, ch 2, 2 sc) in same sp, *sc in next st, (sc in next ch sp, sc in next st) 15 times, (sc, ch 2, sc) in next ch-2 sp, sc in next st, (sc in next ch sp, sc in next st) 15 times*, (2 sc, ch 2, 2 sc) in next end ch sp; repeat between **, join, fasten off.

Diamond No. 2 (make 11)

Rnds 1-10: Substituting gray for black and black for gray, repeat same rnds of Diamond No. 1.

Rnd 11: With gray, work rnd 11 of Diamond No. 1, **do not** fasten off.

Rnd 12: Working in sps between dc and

cls, sl st in next sp, ch 1, 2 sc in same sp, 2 sc in next sp, *(2 sc, ch 2, 2 sc) in next end ch sp, 2 sc in each of next 12 sps, (sc, ch 1, sc) in next ch-3 sp*, 2 sc in each of next 12 sps*; repeat between **, 2 sc in each of last 10 sps, join with sl st in first sc.

Rnd 13: Ch 3, dc in same st, (skip next st, 2 dc in next st) 2 times, *(2 tr, ch 2, 2 tr) in next end ch sp, skip next 2 sts, 2 dc in next st, (skip next st, 2 dc in next st) 12 times, (dc, ch 2, dc) in next ch-1 sp*, (skip next st, 2 dc in next st) 13 times; repeat between **, (skip next st, 2 dc in next st) 10 times, join with sl st in top of ch-3.

Rnd 14: Sl st in sp between first 2 sts, ch 1, sc in same sp, (ch 1, sc in sp between next 2 dc) 2 times, *ch 1, sc in sp between next 2 tr, ch 2, (hdc, ch 3, hdc) in next end ch sp, ch 2, sc in sp between next 2 tr, (ch 1, sc in sp between next 2 dc) 13 times, ch 1, skip next st, (hdc, ch 2, hdc) in next ch sp, skip next st*, (ch 1, sc in sp between next 2 dc) 13 times; repeat between **, (ch 1, sc in sp between next 2 dc) 10 times, ch 1, join with sl st in first sc.

Rnd 15: Sl st in next ch sp, ch 1, sc in same ch sp, *sc in next st, (sc in next ch sp, sc in next st) 3 times, *(2 sc, ch 2, 2 sc) in next end ch sp, sc in next st, (sc in next ch sp, sc in next st) 15 times, (sc, ch 2, sc) in next ch-2 sp, sc in next st*, (sc in next ch sp, sc in next st) 15 times; repeat between **, (sc in next ch sp, sc in next st) 11 times, join, fasten off.

Diamond No. 3 (make 7)

Rnd 1: With gray, ch 5, sl st in first ch to form ring, ch 1, 12 sc in ring, join with sl st in first sc (12 sc).

Rnd 2: Working this rnd in **back lps** only, ch 1, sc in first 5 sts, (2 sc, ch 1, 2 sc) in next st, sc in next 5 sts, (2 sc, ch 1, 2 sc) in last st, join.

Rnd 3: Ch 1, sc in first st, sc in **back lp** of next st, *(sc, ch 1, sc) in next st, (sc in **back lp** of next st, sc in next st) 2 times, (sc, ch 1, sc) in **back lp** of next ch-1*, (sc in next st, sc in **back lp** of next st) 2 times; repeat between **, sc in next st, sc in **back lp** of last st, join (24 sc, 4 ch sps).

Rnd 4: Ch 1, sc in each of first 3 sts, sc in next ch sp, sc in next 6 sts, (sc, ch 1, sc) in next ch sp, sc in next 6 sts, sc in next ch sp, sc in next 6 sts, (sc, ch 1, sc) in next ch sp, sc in each of last 3 sts, join.

Rnd 5: Ch 1, sc in **back lp** of first st, lsc, *sc in **back lp** of next st, (lsc, ch 1, lsc) in next ch-1 sp on rnd before last, (sc in **back lp** of next st, lsc) 3 times, sc in **back lp** of next st, (sc, ch 1, sc) in next ch sp*, (sc in **back lp** of next st, lsc) 3 times; repeat between **, (sc in **back lp** of next st, lsc) 2 times, join.

Rnd 6: Ch 3, *dc in each st across to next ch sp, (dc, ch 1, dc) in next ch sp, dc in each st across to next ch sp, (2 dc, ch 3, 2 dc) in next ch sp; repeat from *, dc in each st across, join with sl st in top of ch-3.

Rnd 7: Ch 1, sc in first st, (ch 1, skip next st, sc in next st) 2 times, *ch 1, (hdc, ch 2, hdc) in next ch sp, (ch 1, skip next st, sc in next st) 6 times, ch 1, (sc, hdc, ch 1, hdc, sc) in next ch sp*, (ch 1, skip next st, sc in next st) 6 times; repeat between **, (ch 1, skip next st, sc in next st) 3 times, ch 1, skip last st, join.

Rnd 8: Ch 1, sc in first st, (ldc, sc in next st) 2 times, *ldc in next end ch sp on rnd before last, skip next hdc, (sc, ch 1, sc) in next ch-2 sp, skip next hdc, ldc in same ch-1 sp on rnd before last as last ldc, (sc in next st, ldc) 5 times, sc in next st, ldc in end ch-3 sp on rnd before last, sc in next sc, sc in next hdc, (hdc, ch 2, hdc) in next end ch sp, sc in next hdc, sc in next sc, ldc in same end ch-3 sp on rnd before last*, (sc in next st, ldc) 5 times, sc in next st; repeat between **, (sc in next st, ldc) 3 times, join.

Rnd 9: Ch 1, sc in first st, (ch 1, skip next st, sc in next st) 3 times, *ch 1, sc in next ch-1 sp, ch 1, (sc in next sc, ch 1, skip next ldc) 7 times, sc in next sc, ch 1, skip next sc, sc in next hdc, ch 1, (sc, ch 1, sc) in next end ch sp, ch 1, sc in next hdc, ch 1, skip next sc*, (sc in next sc, ch 1, skip next ldc) 7 times, sc in next sc; repeat between **, (sc in next sc, ch 1, skip next ldc) 4 times, join.

Rnd 10: Ch 1, sc in **back lp** of first st, (ldc, sc in **back lp** of next st) 3 times, *sc in next ch sp, ch 1, sc in **back lp** of next st, ch 1, sc in next ch sp, (sc in **back lp** of next st, ldc) 8 times, sc in **back lp** of next st, hdc in next ch sp, skip next st, (dc, ch 3, dc) in next end ch sp, skip next st, hdc in next ch sp*, (sc in **back lp** of next st, ldc) 8 times, sc in **back lp** of next st; repeat between **, (sc in **back lp** of next st, ldc) 5 times, join, fasten off.

Rnds 11-15: Repeat same rnds of Diamond No. 2.

Assembly

To **join,** hold two Diamonds wrong sides together, matching sts; working through both

Continued on page 126

Challenger

rosalie de vries, designer

Strategy reigns in the creation of this stunning afghan. A special challenge for the advanced crocheter, you'll savor the completion of this adventurous throw.

Finished Size
42" x 60" without fringe

Materials
Worsted-weight yarn — 12½ oz. black, 12 oz. gray, 10½ oz. blue and 9½ oz. white; G crochet hook or size needed to obtain gauge.

Gauge
4 dc sts = 1"; 2 dc rows = 1".

Skill Level

★★★★ Extra challenging

Instructions
Afghan
Note: **Do not** turn at end of each row.

Row 1: With black, ch 8, dc in 4th ch from hook, dc in next 4 chs, (ch 15, dc in 4th ch from hook, dc in next 4 chs — see photo on pg. 126 — leaving last 7 chs unworked) 19 times, fasten off (20 columns, 19 ch-7 sps).

Row 2: Join blue with sl st in first ch of first ch 3, ch 5, dc in 4th ch from hook, dc in next ch, skip next ch of ch-3, sl st in next ch, *ch 3, dc in next 5 dc, skip next 2 chs of ch-7, sl st in next ch, ch 1, skip next ch, sl st in next ch, skip next 2 chs; working on opposite side of chs at bottom of dcs, dc in next 5 chs, ch 3, sl st in first ch of next ch-3, ch 5, dc in 4th ch from hook, dc in next ch, skip next ch of ch-3, sl st in next ch; repeat from * across, fasten off.

Note: For **reverse sl st,** working from left to right, insert hook in next sc to the right, yo, draw loop through st and lp on hook.

Row 3: Join gray with sl st in first ch of first ch-3, ch 8, dc in 4th ch from hook, dc in next 4 chs, skip next ch of ch-3, sl st in next ch, *ch 3, dc in each of next 2 dc, sl st in top of next ch-3, sc in next 5 dc, sl st in next ch-1 sp, (sc in next dc on next column, reverse sl st in corresponding sc on last column) 5 times, sl st in first ch of next ch-3; working on opposite side of chs at bottom of dcs, dc in each of next 2 chs, ch 3, sl st in first ch of next ch-3, ch 8, dc in 4th ch from hook, dc in next 4 chs, skip next ch of ch-3, sl st in next ch; repeat from * across, fasten off.

Row 4: Join white with sl st in first ch of first ch-3, ch 5, dc in 4th ch from hook, dc in next ch, skip next ch of ch-3, sl st in next ch, *ch 3, dc in next 5 dc, sl st in top of next ch-3, sc in each of next 2 dc, (sc in next dc on next column, reverse sl st in corresponding sc on last column) 2 times, sl st in first ch of next ch-3; working on opposite side of chs at bottom of dcs, dc in next 5 chs, ch 3, sl st in first ch of next ch-3, ch 5, dc in 4th ch from hook, dc in next ch, skip next ch of ch-3, sl st in next ch; repeat from * across, fasten off.

Row 5: Join black with sl st in first ch of first ch-3, ch 8, dc in 4th ch from hook, dc in next 4 chs, skip next ch of ch-3, sl st in next ch, *ch 3, dc in each of next 2 dc, sl st in top of next ch-3, sc in next 5 dc, (sc in next dc on next column, reverse sl st in corresponding sc on last column) 5 times, sl st in first ch of next ch-3; working on opposite side of chs at bottom of dcs, dc in each of next 2 chs, ch 3, sl st in first ch of next ch-3, ch 8, dc in 4th ch from hook, dc in next 4 chs, skip next ch of ch-3, sl st in next ch; repeat from * across, fasten off.

Continued on page 126

Challenger

Continued from page 124

Rows 6-45: Working in color sequence of blue, gray, white, black, repeat rows 4 and 5 alternately.

Row 46: Join blue with sl st in top of first ch-3, *[ch 3, dc in next 5 sts, sl st in top of next ch-3, sc in each of next 2 dc, (sc in next dc on next column, reverse sl st in corresponding sc on last column) 2 times, sl st in first ch of next ch-3; working on opposite side of chs at bottom of dcs, dc in next 5 chs, ch 3, sl st in first ch of next ch-3, fasten off], skip next ch of ch-3, join with sl st in next ch; repeat from * 17 more times; repeat between [ ].

Row 47: Join gray with sc in first blue dc between first 2 columns, sc in next 4 dc, (sc in next dc on next column, reverse sl st in corresponding sc on last column) 5 times, sl st in first ch of next ch-3, fasten off. Repeat between remaining columns.

Row 48: Join black with sl st in end of first black column, (ch 2, sl st in end of next row) across, fasten off.

Border
Working in sts on one long edge of Afghan, join black with sc in last st, **reverse sc** *(see fig. 10, pg. 159)* in each st across, fasten off.

Repeat on other long edge of afghan.

Fringe
For **each Fringe,** cut one strand of each

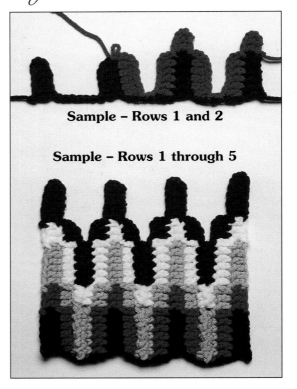

Sample – Rows 1 and 2

Sample – Rows 1 through 5

color 10" long. With all strands held together, fold in half, insert hook in row or sp, draw fold through row or sp, draw all loose ends through fold, tighten. Trim ends. Fringe in each ch sp or end of row on each short end of Afghan.✤

Contemporary Diamonds

Continued from page 123

thickness, join black with sc in ch sp, (ch 2, skip next st, sc in next st) 16 times, ch 2, skip next 2 sts, sc in next ch sp.

Join Diamonds at random according to Assembly Diagram.

Border
Working in **front lps** only, join black with sc in any st, ch 2, skip next st or ch, (sc in next st or ch, ch 2, skip next st or ch or seam) around with ch-3 at points, join with sl st in first sc, fasten off.

Tassel (make 8)
For each Tassel, cut 30 strands black each 16" long. Tie separate strand tightly around middle of all strands; fold in half. Wrap 20" strand around folded strands 1" from fold, secure. Trim ends.

Tie one Tassel to each ch-3 on each short end of afghan.✤

Continued from page 118

Rows 171-183: Repeat same rows of Strip No. 1.

Row 184: Join navy with sc in first ch sp; to **join** to last Strip made, ch 2, drop lp from hook, pull lp through corresponding ch sp on other Strip from bottom to top, ch 1; sc in same ch sp as last sc on this Strip, (sc in next ch sp, join, sc in same ch sp) across, fasten off.

Strip No. 3

Rows 1-170: Working in color sequence of teal, coral, teal, dk. purple, teal, coral, teal, lt. blue, teal, lt. purple, teal, med. blue, teal, dk. purple, teal, dk. red, teal, repeat same rows of Strip No. 1.

Rows 171-183: Repeat same rows of Strip No. 1.

Row 184: Repeat same row of Strip No. 2.

Strip No. 4

Rows 1-170: Working in color sequence of med. blue, teal, lt. blue, teal, dk. red, teal, med. blue, teal, dk. purple, teal, dk. red, teal, lt. blue, teal, coral, teal, lt. purple, repeat same rows of Strip No. 1.

Rows 171-183: Repeat same rows of Strip No. 1.

Row 184: Repeat same row of Strip No. 2.

Strip No. 5

Rows 1-170: Working in color sequence of teal, dk. red, teal, lt. purple, teal, dk. purple, teal, coral, teal, lt. blue, teal, coral, teal, lt. purple, teal, med. blue, teal, repeat same rows of Strip No. 1.

Rows 171-176: Repeat same rows of Strip No. 1.

Rows 177-182: Repeat rows 178-183 of Strip No. 1

Row 183: Repeat row 184 of Strip No. 2.

Border

Rnd 1: With right side facing you, join navy with sc in first sc of row 176 on Strip No. 5; for **corner,** ch 2; sc in same st, (sc, ch 2, sc) in each ch-2 sp across with (sc, ch 2, sc) in last st for corner, (sc, ch 2, sc) in end of next row, skip next 2 rows, (sc, ch 2, sc) in end of next row, [(sc, ch 2, sc) in next 5 ch-1 sps, *skip next row, (sc, ch 2, sc) in end of next row*; repeat between ** 5 more times]; repeat between [ ] 3 more times, (sc, ch 2, sc) in next 5 ch-1 sps; repeat between ** 2 more times; for **corner,** (sc, ch 2, sc) in next sc; (sc, ch 2, sc) in each ch-2 sp across with (sc, ch 2, sc) in last sc for corner, (sc, ch 2, sc) in end of next row, skip next 2 rows,

(sc, ch 2, sc) in end of next row, skip next row; ◊working in starting ch on opposite side of row 1 on same Strip, (sc, ch 2, sc) in first ch and every other ch across; repeat between ** 6 more times◊; repeat between ◊◊ 3 more times; working in starting ch on opposite side of row 1 on last Strip, (sc, ch 2, sc) in first ch and in every other ch across; repeat between ** 2 more times, join with sl st in first sc (280 ch sps).

Rnd 2: Sl st in next ch sp, (sc, ch 2, sc, ch 3, sc, ch 2, sc) in same ch sp, (sc, ch 2, sc) in each ch sp around with (sc, ch 2, sc, ch 3, sc, ch 2, sc) in each corner ch sp, join, fasten off.

Rnd 3: Join dk. red with sc in first ch-2 sp after any corner ch-3 sp, *[(3 dc in next ch-2 sp, sc in next ch-2 sp) across to next corner ch-3 sp, 5 dc in next ch sp], sc in next ch sp; repeat from * 2 more times; repeat between [ ], join, **turn.**

Rnd 4: Ch 3, 2 dc in same st, *[skip next dc, sc in next dc, 5 dc in next dc, sc in next dc, skip next dc], 3 dc in next sc, (sc in center st of next 3-dc group, 3 dc in next sc) across to next corner; repeat from * 2 more times; repeat between [ ], (3 dc in next sc, sc in center st of next 3-dc group) across, join with sl st in top of ch-3, **turn.**

Rnd 5: Ch 2, *dc in next sc, (hdc in next dc, sc in next dc, hdc in next dc, dc in next sc) across to next corner 5-dc group, hdc in each of next 2 dc, (sc, ch 3, sc) in next dc, hdc in each of next 2 dc; repeat from * 3 more times, dc in next sc, hdc in next dc, sc in next dc, join with sl st in top of ch-2, **do not** turn, fasten off.

Rnd 6: Join teal with sc in first hdc after any corner ch-3 sp, ch 2, sc in same st, skip next st, [*(sc, ch 2, sc) in next st, skip next st; repeat from * across to next corner ch sp, (sc, ch 2, sc, ch 3, sc, ch 2, sc) in next corner ch sp, skip next st]; repeat between [ ] 3 more times, join.

Rnd 7: Sl st into next ch-2 sp, ch 3, 2 dc in same sp, *sc in next ch-2 sp, (3 dc in next ch-2 sp, sc in next ch-2 sp) across to next corner ch-3 sp, 5 dc in next corner ch sp; repeat from * 3 more times, sc in next ch sp, join with sl st in top of ch-3, **turn.**

Rnd 8: Sl st in next sc, repeat rnd 4.

Rnd 9: Repeat rnd 5.

Rnd 10: With navy, repeat rnd 6, fasten off.

Rnd 11: Join med. blue with sc in any ch-2 sp, ch 2, sc in same sp, (sc, ch 2, sc) in each ch-2 sp around with (sc, ch 3, sc) in each corner ch-3 sp, join, fasten off.✱

Fun & Fancy

Return to a carefree time of delight and whimsy with magical designs that capture the essence of gaiety and light-heartedness. Filled with a rainbow of colors and styles, fun and adventure await you in this fairyland of fanciful dreams and festive cheer.

Rainbow Ripple

jo ann maxwell, designer

They'll adore this traditional white ripple embossed with bands of brightly hued popcorns. Add a dash of color to your child's room with this vivid accent.

Finished Size
47½" x 67½"

Materials
Worsted-weight yarn — 35 oz. white, 7 oz. each red, coral, yellow, green, turquoise and purple; J crochet hook or size needed to obtain gauge.

Gauge
5 dc sts = 2"; 2 dc rows = 1½".

Skill Level
★ Easy

Instructions
Afghan

Notes: To **dc next 3 sts tog,** (yo, insert hook in next st, yo, draw lp through, yo, draw through 2 lps on hook) 3 times, yo, draw through all 4 lps on hook.

For **shell,** 5 dc in next ch or st.

For **reverse shell,** (yo, insert hook in next st, yo, draw lp through, yo, draw through 2 lps on hook) 5 times, yo, draw through all 6 lps on hook.

Row 1: With white, ch 173, dc 4th, 5th and 6th chs from hook tog, dc in next 9 chs, shell, dc in next 9 chs, (reverse shell over next 5 chs, dc in next 9 chs, shell, dc in next 9 chs) across to last 4 chs, dc next 3 chs tog, dc in last ch, turn. Front of row 1 is right side of work.

Rows 2-3: Working these rows in **back lps** *(see fig. 1, pg. 158),* ch 3, dc next 3 sts tog, dc in next 9 sts, shell, dc in next 9 sts, (reverse shell, dc in next 9 sts, shell, dc in next 9 sts) across to last 4 sts, dc next 3 sts tog, dc in last st, turn. At end of last row, **do not** turn, fasten off.

Note: For **popcorn stitch (pc),** 5 dc in next st, drop lp from hook, insert hook in first st of 5-dc group, pick up dropped lp, draw through st.

Row 4: With right side facing you, working this row in **back lps,** join red with sl st in first st, ch 3, dc next 3 sts tog, pc, (dc in next st, pc) 4 times, (2 dc, pc, 2 dc) in next st, pc, (dc in next st, pc) 4 times, *reverse shell, pc, (dc in next st, pc) 4 times, (2 dc, pc, 2 dc) in next st, pc, (dc in next st, pc) 4 times; repeat from * across to last 4 sts, dc next 3 sts tog, dc in last st, **do not** turn, fasten off.

Row 5: Working this row in **both lps,** join white with sl st in first st, repeat row 2, fasten off.

Rows 6-15: Working in color sequence of coral, white, yellow, white, green, white, turquoise, white, purple, white, repeat rows 4 and 5 alternately. At end of last row, turn, **do not** fasten off.

Rows 16-49: Repeat row 2. At end of last row, **do not** turn, fasten off.

Rows 50-61: Following color sequence of purple, white, turquoise, white, green, white, yellow, white, coral, white, red, white, repeat rows 4 and 5 alternately. At end of last row, turn, **do not** fasten off.

Rows 62-63: Repeat row 2. At end of last row, fasten off.✤

Ribbons & Lace

roberta maier, designer

Crocheted ribbons woven through lacy strips create a lovely textured effect that exudes patriotic charm with its red, white and blue color scheme. Hats off to this exciting design!

Finished Size
48" x 68"

Materials
Worsted-weight yarn — 32½ oz. white, 17 oz. navy and 11 oz. red; 2 safety pins; G crochet hook or size needed to obtain gauge.

Gauge
4 sc sts = 1"; 4 sc rows = 1".

Skill Level
★ Easy

Instructions
Strip (make 9)
Lace Section
Row 1: With white, ch 17, 2 dc in 6th ch from hook, ch 2, 2 dc in next ch, ch 2, skip next 2 chs, sc in next ch, ch 2, skip next 2 chs, 2 dc in next ch, ch 2, 2 dc in next ch, skip next 2 chs, dc in last ch, turn (10 dc, 1 sc).

Note: For **shell,** (2 dc, ch 2, 2 dc) in next ch sp.

Row 2: Ch 3, shell in next ch sp, ch 5, skip next 2 ch sps, shell in next ch sp, dc in last st, turn.

Row 3: Ch 3, shell in ch sp of next shell, ch 2, sc in 3rd ch of next ch-5, ch 2, shell in ch sp of next shell, dc in last st, turn.

Rows 4-105: Repeat rows 2 and 3 alternately. At end of last row, fasten off.

Ribbon Section
Row 1: With navy, ch 6, sc in 2nd ch from hook, sc in each ch across, turn (5 sc).

Rows 2-259: Ch 1, sc in each st across, turn. At end of last row, fasten off.

Matching first row on each, weave Ribbon Section through ch sps of Lace Section; temporarily secure ends with safety pins.

Edging
Rnd 1: Working in ends of rows on Lace Section, join red with sl st in end of last row, ch 3, (2 dc, ch 2, 3 dc) in same row, 2 dc in end of each row across to last row, (3 dc, ch 2, 3 dc) in last row; working in starting ch on opposite side of row 1, hdc in ch at base of next 2 dc, hdc in next ch; working through both thicknesses of Lace Strip and starting ch on Ribbon Strip, sc in next ch on Lace Strip and first ch on Ribbon Strip, skip next ch on both Strips, (hdc, 3 dc, ch 2, 3 dc, hdc) in next ch on both Strips, skip next ch on both Strips, sc in next ch on both Strips; working on Lace Strip only, hdc in each of next 2 chs, (3 dc, ch 2, 3 dc) in end of next row, 2 dc in each row across to last row, (3 dc, ch 2, 3 dc) in last row, skip next 2 dc, hdc in each of next 2 dc; working through both thicknesses of Lace Strip and Ribbon Strip, sc in next ch on Lace Strip and first st on Ribbon Strip, skip next ch or st on both Strips, (hdc, 3 dc, ch 2, 3 dc, hdc) in next st or ch on both Strips, skip next ch or st on both Strips, sc in next ch or st on both Strips, hdc in each of next 2 dc on Lace Strip only, join with sl st in top of ch-3, fasten off.

Notes: For **double treble crochet (dtr)** *(see fig. 8, pg. 159),* yo 3 times, insert hook in ch sp, yo, draw lp through, (yo, draw through 2 lps on hook) 4 times.

For **picot,** ch 3, sl st in top of last st made.

Continued on page 140

Floral Delight

sandra miller-maxfield, designer

Big bold flowers on a lush carpet of aqua make this pleasing afghan a real winner. It's chic and modern, and the eyelets add an interesting touch.

Finished Size
53" x 59" without Fringe

Materials
Worsted-weight yarn — 40 oz. aqua, 3½ oz. each pink and blue, 2 oz. yellow; tapestry needle; I crochet hook or size needed to obtain gauge.

Gauge
3 dc sts = 1"; 5 dc rows = 3".

Skill Level
★ Easy

Instructions

Afghan

Row 1: With aqua, ch 161, dc in 4th ch from hook, dc in each ch across, turn (159 dc).

Row 2: Ch 3, dc same st and next st tog, (ch 1, skip next st, dc in next 10 sts) 14 times, ch 1, skip next st, dc in each of last 2 sts, turn.

Row 3: Ch 3, dc same st and next st tog, dc in next ch, (ch 1, skip next st, dc in next 10 sts or chs) 14 times, dc in each of last 2 sts, turn.

Row 4: Ch 3, dc same st and next st tog, (dc in each st across to one st before next ch sp, ch 1, skip next st, dc in next ch) 14 times, dc in each st across, turn.

Row 5: Ch 3, dc same st and next st tog, (dc in each st across to next ch sp, dc in next ch, ch 1, skip next st) 14 times, dc in each st across, turn.

Rows 6-12: Repeat rows 4 and 5 alternately, ending with row 4.

Row 13: Ch 3, dc same st and next st tog, ch 1, skip next st, (dc in each st across to next ch sp, dc in next ch, ch 1, skip next st) 14 times, dc in each st across, turn.

Row 14: Ch 3, dc same st and next st tog, dc in next ch, (dc in each st across to one st before next ch sp, ch 1, skip next st, dc in next ch) 14 times, dc in each st across, turn.

Rows 15-22: Repeat rows 5 and 4 alternately.

Row 23: Repeat row 13.

Row 24: Ch 3, dc same st and next st tog, ch 1, skip next st, dc in next ch, (dc in each st across to one st before next ch sp, ch 1, skip next st, dc in next ch) 14 times, dc in each st across, turn.

Rows 25-33: Repeat rows 5 and 4 alternately, ending with row 5.

Row 34: Ch 3, dc same st and next st tog, (dc in each st across to one st before next ch sp, ch 1, skip next st, dc in next ch) 14 times, dc in next 9 sts, ch 1, skip next st, dc in each of last 2 sts, turn.

Row 35: Ch 3, dc same st and next st tog, dc in next ch, ch 1, skip next st, (dc in each st across to next ch sp, dc in next ch, ch 1, skip next st) 14 times, dc in each st across, turn.

Rows 36-44: Repeat rows 4 and 5 alternately, ending with row 4.

Row 45: Repeat row 13.

Row 46: Repeat row 24.

Row 47: Ch 3, dc same st and next st tog, (dc in each st across to next ch sp, dc in next ch, ch 1, skip next st) 14 times, dc in next 9 sts, dc in next ch, dc in each of last 2 sts, turn.

Continued on page 141

Granny's Sweetheart

sandra miller-maxfield, designer

Granny pulled out her yarn bag and made her little sweetheart a warm and cozy cover to snuggle under. Each block is adorned with a lacy heart to reflect a dear one's love.

Finished Size
46½" x 64½"

Materials
Worsted-weight yarn — 57 oz. variegated, 24 oz. purple and 3½ oz. white; safety or bobbie pin for marker; tapestry needle; H crochet hook or size needed to obtain gauge.

Gauge
7 dc sts = 2"; 3 dc rows = 2".
Each Block is 9" square.

Skill Level
★★ Average

Instructions
Block (make 35)
Heart

Row 1: With purple, ch 3, 3 hdc in 3rd ch from hook, turn (4 hdc).

Row 2: Ch 2, hdc in next st, 2 hdc in next st, hdc in last st, turn (5).

Rows 3-5: Ch 2, 2 hdc in next st, hdc in each st across with 2 hdc in last st, turn (7, 9, 11).

Row 6: For **first side,** ch 2, 2 hdc in next st, hdc in next 4 sts leaving remaining sts unworked, turn (7).

Row 7: Ch 1, sc in first st, (sc next 2 sts tog) 3 times, turn, fasten off (4).

Row 6: For **2nd side,** join with sl st in next unworked st on row 5, ch 2, hdc in same st, hdc in each of next 3 sts, 2 hdc in last st, turn.

Row 7: Repeat row 7 of first side.

Background

Row 1: Working in ends of rows and in sts around outer edge of Heart, join purple with sc in end of row 6 on first side at center of Heart, sc in next row, sc in first st on row 7, 2 sc in each of next 3 sts, sc in end of row 7, 2 sc in each of next 5 rows, sc in end of next row, sc in starting ch on opposite side of row 1, sc in end of same row, 2 sc in each of next 4 rows, sc in each of next 2 rows, sc in next st, 2 sc in each of next 3 sts, sc in end of row 7 (mark last st made), sc in end of next row, fasten off (42 sc).

Row 2: Working this row in **back lps** *(see fig. 1, pg. 158),* join variegated with sl st in marked st, skip last st, (2 dc, ch 3, 2 dc) in first st of row 1, skip next st, sl st in next st, fasten off.

Rnd 3: Working this rnd in **back lps,** join variegated with sl st in 22nd st of row 1 at tip of heart, (ch 3, 2 dc, ch 3, 3 dc) in same st, skip next 4 sts, 3 dc in next st, skip next 4 sts, (3 dc, ch 3, 2 dc) in next st, skip next st; hdc in next st, skip next 2 sts, sc in each of next 3 sts, skip next st, (3 dc, ch 3, 3 dc) in ch-3 sp of row 2, skip next st on row 1, sc in each of next 3 sts, skip next 2 sts, hdc in next st, skip next st, (2 dc, ch 3, 3 dc) in next st, skip next 4 sts, 3 dc in next st, skip last 4 sts, join with sl st in top of ch-3.

Rnds 4-5: Ch 3, dc in each st around with (2 dc, ch 3, 2 dc) in each ch sp, join. At end of last rnd (68 dc, 4 ch sps), fasten off.

Rnd 6: Join purple with sl st in any st, repeat rnd 4, fasten off (84 dc, 4 ch sps).

Rnd 7: Join variegated with sl st in any st, repeat rnd 4, fasten off (100 dc, 4 ch sps).

Continued on page 140

Tropical Lagoon

sandra miller-maxfield, designer

Brilliant South Sea fish swim gracefully along on this island delight. The lacy background is light and airy, yet warm enough to ward off cool breezes.

Finished Size
39" x 58"

Materials
Worsted-weight yarn — 42 oz. pink, small amount each turquoise, orange, green and blue; size 35 broomstick lace pin; H crochet hook or size needed to obtain gauge.

Gauge
1 row = 1"

Skill Level
★★ Average

Instructions

Afghan

Row 1: With pink, ch 170, **do not** turn, slip last lp on hook onto broomstick; working back towards slip knot, *insert hook in next ch, yo, draw lp through ch and slip onto broomstick (see ill. No. 1); repeat from * across, **do not** turn; ◊slip first 5 lps from broomstick onto hook, yo, draw lp through all 5 lps on hook (see ill. No. 2), ch 1, 5 sc (see ill. No. 3) in same 5-lp group, (slip next 5 lps from broomstick onto hook, yo, draw lp

through all 5 lps, yo, draw lp through both lps on hook, 4 sc in same 5-lp group) across◊, **do not** turn.

Rows 2-56: Slip last lp on hook onto broomstick, (insert hook in next st, yo, draw lp through st and slip onto broomstick) across; repeat between ◊◊ on row 1. At end of last row, fasten off.

Edging
Note: For **V-st,** (dc, ch 1, dc) in next st.

Join pink with sc in first st of first 5-sc group, skip next st, 5 dc in next st, skip next st, sc in each of next 2 sts, (ch 1, skip next st, V-st in next st, ch 1, skip next st, sc in each of next 2 sts) 32 times, skip next st, 5 dc in next st, ch 1, skip next st, sc in next st; working in sc at end of rows, (ch 1, V-st in next sc, ch 1, sc

Continued on page 140

BROOMSTICK LACE

No. 1

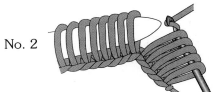

No. 2

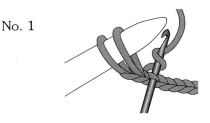

No. 3

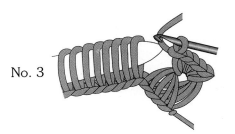

Tropical Lagoon

Continued from page 139

in next sc) 27 times, ch 1, V-st in next sc; working on opposite side of starting ch, ch 1, sc in first ch, skip next ch, 5 dc in next ch, ch 1, skip next ch, sc in each of next 2 chs, (ch 1, skip next ch, V-st in next ch, ch 1, skip next ch, sc in each of next 2 chs) across to last 4 chs, skip next ch, 5 dc in next ch, ch 1, skip next ch, sc in last ch; working in sc at ends of rows, ch 1, V-st in next sc, (ch 1, sc in next sc, ch 1, V-st in next sc) 27 times, ch 1, join with sl st in first sc, fasten off.

Fish (make 1 turquoise, 1 orange, 1 green, 1 blue)
Row 1: Ch 4, 4 dc in 4th ch from hook, turn (5 dc).

Row 2: Ch 3, dc in same st, 2 dc in each st across, turn (10).

Row 3: Ch 3, 2 dc in next st, (dc in next st, 2 dc in next st) across, turn (15).

Row 4: (Ch 5, skip next 2 sts, sc in next st) 4 times, ch 2, dc in last st, turn (5 ch sps).

Rows 5-6: (Ch 5, sc in next ch sp) across to last ch sp, ch 2, dc in last ch sp, turn.

Row 7: Ch 5, sc in next ch sp, ch 2, dc in last ch sp, turn.

Row 8: Ch 2, dc in last ch sp, turn.

Row 9: (Ch 5, sc in 2nd ch from hook, sc in each of next 3 chs), dc in ch sp on row 8; repeat between ( ), sl st in end of row 8, fasten off.

Sew Fish across one end of Afghan.❖

Ribbons & Lace

Continued from page 132

Rnd 2: Join white with sc in 2nd st, sc in next st, *3 sc in next ch sp, sc in each st across to next ch sp, 3 sc in next ch sp, sc in each of next 2 sts, skip next 8 sts, (dtr, picot) 12 times in next ch sp, dtr in same sp, skip next 8 sts*, sc in each of next 2 sts; repeat between **, join with sl st in first sc, fasten off.

Assembly
To **join** Strips, hold two Strips wrong sides together, matching sts; working through both thicknesses, join white with sl st in 6th sc after last dtr on one end, ch 1, (sl st in next st, ch 1) across to 7th st before dtr on opposite end, sl st in next st, fasten off.

Repeat with remaining Strips.❖

Granny's Sweetheart

Continued from page 137

Rnd 8: Working in **front lps** of rnd 1, join white with sc in st at tip of heart, ch 3, dc in same st, skip next st, *(sc, ch 3, dc) in next st, skip next st; repeat from * around, join with sl st in first sc, fasten off.

Hold Blocks wrong sides together, matching sts; working in **back lps,** sew Blocks together in five rows of seven Blocks each.

Edging
Working around entire outer edge, join variegated with sl st in any st, ch 3, dc in each st, dc in each seam and 2 dc in ch sp on each side of seam around with 5 dc in each corner ch sp, join with sl st in top of ch-3, fasten off.❖

Floral Delight

Continued from page 134

Rows 48-55: Repeat rows 4 and 5 alternately.

Row 56: Repeat row 34.

Row 57: Repeat row 35.

Row 58: Repeat row 14.

Rows 59-66: Repeat rows 5 and 4 alternately.

Row 67: Repeat row 13.

Row 68: Repeat row 24.

Row 69: Repeat row 47.

Rows 70-78: Repeat rows 4 and 5 alternately, ending with row 4.

Row 79: Repeat row 13.

Row 80: Repeat row 14.

Rows 81-89: Repeat rows 5 and 4 alternately, ending with row 5.

Row 90: Repeat row 24.

Row 91: Ch 3, dc same st and next st tog, dc in next ch, ch 1, skip next st, (dc in each st across to next ch sp, dc in next ch, ch 1, skip next st) 13 times, dc in next 9 sts, dc in next ch, dc in each of last 2 sts, turn.

Rows 92-97: Repeat rows 4 and 5 alternately.

Row 98: Ch 3, dc in each st and in each ch across, turn.

Row 99: Ch 1, sc in each st across, turn, fasten off.

Flower (make 3 blue, 3 pink)

Row 1: With yellow, ch 6, sc in 2nd ch

LOOP STITCH

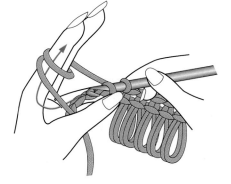

from hook, sc in each ch across, turn (5 sc).

Note: **For loop stitch (lp st)** *(see ill.),* wrap yarn around two fingers 2 times, insert hook in next st and through lps on fingers, draw lps through, yo, draw though all lps on hook.

Row 2: Ch 1, lp st in each st across, turn.

Row 3: Ch 1, 2 sc in first st, sc in each st across with 2 sc in last st, turn (7).

Row 4: Ch 1, lp st in each st across, turn.

Row 5: Ch 1, sc first 2 sts tog, sc in each st across to last 2 sts, sc last 2 sts tog, turn (5).

Row 6: Ch 1, lp st in each st across, **do not** turn.

Rnd 7: Working around outer edge in ends of rows and sts, evenly space 30 lp sts around, join with sl st in first lp st, fasten off.

Row 8: Working in rows, for **petal,** with loops facing you, join flower color with sl st in any st, ch 2, hdc in same st, hdc in next 5 sts, turn (7 hdc).

Row 9: Ch 2, 2 hdc in next st, hdc in each st across with 2 hdc in last st, turn (9).

Row 10: Ch 2, hdc in each st across, turn.

Rows 11-13: Repeat rows 9 and 10 alternately, ending with row 9 and 13 sts.

Rows 14-15: Ch 2, hdc next 2 sts tog, hdc in each st across to last 2 sts, hdc last 2 sts tog, turn (11, 9).

Row 16: Ch 2, (hdc next 2 sts tog) across, turn (5).

Row 17: Ch 2, hdc 2nd st and last st tog, fasten off.

Joining in next st on rnd 7, repeat rows 8-17 of petal 4 more times.

Sew one blue and two pink Flowers to one end of Afghan. Sew remaining flowers to opposite end.

Fringe

For **each Fringe,** cut 4 strands of aqua each 16" long. With all four strands held together, fold in half, insert hook in st, draw fold through st, draw all loose ends through fold, tighten. Trim ends.

Fringe in every other st on each short end of Afghan.❖

Beautiful Blocks

Radiating with the opulence of mellow time-polished tiles, multi-colored squares are fitly joined to form a parquetry of crochet. Prized for their convenient versatility, these traditionally styled block creations are the cornerstone of decorating panache.

Bluebells

dorris brooks, designer

Fresh as morning dew on a field of flowers, this beautiful afghan, caressed in shades of blue, will bring warmth and comfort to any room.

Finished Size
47½" x 67"

Materials
Worsted-weight yarn — 22 oz. lt. blue, 18 oz. each dk. blue and white; tapestry needle; I crochet hook or size needed to obtain gauge.

Gauge
2 rnds = 2½" across.
Each Block is 6½" square.

Skill Level
★ Easy

Instructions

Block No. 1 (make 40)
Rnd 1: With dk. blue, ch 4, sl st in first ch to form ring, ch 3, 11 dc in ring, join with sl st in top of ch-3, fasten off (12 dc).

Rnd 2: Join white with sl st in any st, ch 3, dc in same st, 2 dc in each st around, join, fasten off (24).

Rnd 3: Join lt. blue with sl st in any st, (ch 3, 2 dc, ch 2, 3 dc) in same st, ch 5, skip next 5 sts, *(3 dc, ch 2, 3 dc) in next st, ch 5, skip next 5 sts) around, join.

Rnd 4: Sl st in each of next 2 sts, sl st in next ch-2 sp, (ch 3, 2 dc, ch 2, 3 dc) in same sp, *[skip next 2 sts, dc in next st, 5 dc in next ch-5 sp, dc in next st, skip next 2 sts], (3 dc, ch 2, 3 dc) in next ch-2 sp; repeat from * 2 more times; repeat between [ ], join.

Rnd 5: Ch 1, sc in each st around with (sc, ch 2, sc) in each corner ch-2 sp, join with sl st in first sc, fasten off (60 sc, 4 ch-2 sps).

Rnd 6: Join dk. blue with sl st in any corner ch sp, (ch 3, 2 dc, ch 2, 3 dc) in same sp, *[skip next 3 sts, (3 dc in next st, skip next 2 sts) 4 times], (3 dc, ch 2, 3 dc) in next ch-2 sp; repeat from * 2 more times; repeat between [ ], join with sl st in top of ch-3, fasten off.

Block No. 2 (make 30)
Rnd 1: Repeat same rnd of Block No. 1.

Rnd 2: With lt. blue, repeat same rnd of Block No. 1.

Rnds 3-5: With white, repeat same rnds of Block No. 1.

Rnd 6: Repeat same rnd of Block No. 1.

Assembly
Holding Blocks wrong sides together, matching sts, working in **back lps** *(see fig. 1, pg. 158)*, with dk. blue, sew Blocks No. 1 together in four strips of ten Blocks each.

Working in same manner, sew Blocks No. 2 together in three strips of ten Blocks each.

Alternating colors, sew strips together in same manner.

Border
Rnd 1: Working around entire outer edge, join dk. blue with sl st in any corner ch sp, (ch 3, 2 dc, ch 2, 3 dc) in same sp, 3 dc in center dc of each 3-dc group and in each seam around with (3 dc, ch 2, 3 dc) in each corner ch sp, join with sl st in top of ch-3, fasten off.

Rnd 2: Join white with sc in any corner ch-2 sp, (sc, ch 2, 2 sc) in same sp, 4 sc in center st of each 3-dc group around with (2 sc, ch 2, 2 sc) in each corner ch-2 sp, join with sl st in first sc, fasten off.✤

Sugar & Spice

katherine eng, designer

Classic elegance at its finest — that's the only way to describe this marvelous afghan! Its subtle blend of colors and creative use of popcorns make it a real standout.

Finished Size
49" x 65"

Materials
Worsted-weight yarn — 29 oz. ecru, 21 oz. lt. gold and 17 oz. white; tapestry needle; G crochet hook or size needed to obtain gauge.

Gauge
4 sc sts = 1"; 4 sc rows = 1".

Skill Level
★★ Average

Instructions
Strip No. 1
Block (make 10)
Notes: For **beginning popcorn (beg pc)**, ch 3, 4 dc in same st, remove lp from hook, insert hook in top of ch-3, pick up dropped lp, draw through st.

For **popcorn (pc)**, 5 dc in next st, remove lp from hook, insert hook in first st of 5-dc group, pick up dropped lp, draw through st.

Rnd 1: With lt. gold, ch 4, sl st in first ch to form ring, ch 1, 8 sc in ring, join with sl st in first sc (8 sc).

Rnd 2: Beg pc in first st, ch 4, skip next st, (pc in next st, ch 4, skip next st) around, join with sl st in top of first pc, fasten off (4 pc, 4 ch sps).

Rnd 3: Working in front of ch-4, join white with sl st in any unworked sc on rnd 1, (ch 3, 2 dc, ch 3, 3 dc) in same st, ch 1, *(3 dc, ch 3, 3 dc) in next unworked sc, ch 1; repeat from * around, join with sl st in top of ch-3, fasten off.

Rnd 4: Join ecru with sc in any ch-3 sp, ch 1, (3 dc, ch 3, 3 dc) in next ch-1 sp, ch 1, *sc in next ch-3 sp, ch 1, (3 dc, ch 3, 3 dc) in next ch-1 sp, ch 1; repeat from * around, join with sl st in first sc.

Rnd 5: Ch 1, sc in each st and in each ch-1 sp around with (sc, ch 3, sc) in each corner ch-3 sp, join with sl st in first sc, fasten off (44 sc, 4 ch-3 sps).

Rnd 6: Join white with sc in any corner ch-3 sp, ch 3, sc in same sp, *[ch 1, skip next st, (sc in next st, ch 1, skip next st) across to next corner], (sc, ch 3, sc) in next corner ch-3 sp; repeat from * 2 more times; repeat between [ ], join, fasten off.

Rnd 7: Join lt. gold with sl st in any st, ch 3, dc in each ch-1 sp and in each st around with (pc, ch 4, pc) in each corner ch-3 sp, join with sl st in top of ch-3, fasten off.

Rnd 8: Join white with sc in any ch-4 sp, (sc, ch 3, 2 sc) in same sp, *[ch 1, skip next pc, sc in next dc, (ch 1, skip next dc, sc in next dc) across to next corner, ch 1, skip next pc], (2 sc, ch 3, 2 sc) in next ch-4 sp; repeat from * 2 more times; repeat between [ ], join with sl st in first sc, fasten off.

Rnd 9: Join ecru with sc in any st, sc in each ch-1 sp and in each sc around with (sc, ch 3, sc) in each corner ch-3 sp, join, fasten off (21 sc on each side, 4 ch-3 sps).

Holding Blocks wrong sides together, matching sts, with ecru, working in **back lps** *(see fig. 1, pg. 158)*, sew Blocks together to form Strip.

Continued on page 154

Native Sunset

christina mc neese, designer

Like the splendor of a painted sunset this lavish afghan has a look of the Southwest. The raised post stitches add interesting texture to an already beautiful design.

Finished Size
56½" x 67" without fringe

Materials
Fuzzy worsted-weight yarn — 26 oz. white, 17 oz. turquoise and 13 oz. coral; J crochet hook or size needed to obtain gauge.

Gauge
5 dc sts = 2"; 2 dc rows = 1½".
Each Block is 10½" square.

Skill Level
★★ Average

Instructions
Block (make 30)

Rnd 1: With turquoise, ch 6, sl st in first ch to form ring, ch 3, 15 dc in ring, join with sl st in top of ch-3, fasten off (16 dc).

Rnd 2: Join coral with sl st in any st, ch 3, dc in each of next 2 sts, ch 4, skip next st, (dc in each of next 3 sts, ch 4, skip next st) around, join, fasten off.

Rnd 3: Join turquoise with sc in first st, sc in each of next 2 sts; working over ch-4 on last rnd, *(2 tr, ch 3, 2 tr) in next skipped st on rnd before last, sc in each of next 3 sts on this rnd; repeat from * 2 more times, (2 tr, ch 3, 2 tr) in next skipped st on rnd before last, join with sl st in first sc, fasten off.

Rnd 4: Join white with sl st in any ch-3 sp, (ch 3, 2 dc, ch 3, 3 dc) in same sp, dc in next 7 sts, *(3 dc, ch 3, 3 dc) in next ch-3 sp, dc in next 7 sts; repeat from * around, join with sl st in top of ch-3, fasten off.

Note: For **treble front post (tr fp),** yo 2 times, insert hook from front to back around post *(see fig. 9, pg. 159)* of st 3 rnds below; complete as tr.

Rnd 5: Join coral with sl st in any ch-3 sp, (ch 3, 2 dc, ch 3, 3 dc) in same sp, *[dc in next 5 sts, tr fp around each of next 3 sts on rnd 2, skip next 3 sts on this rnd, dc in next 5 sts], (3 dc, ch 3, 3 dc) in next ch-3 sp; repeat from * 2 more times; repeat between [ ], join, fasten off.

Rnd 6: Join turquoise with sl st in first tr fp, ch 3, dc in each of next 2 tr fp, *[sc in next 8 sts, ch 3, skip next ch-3 sp, sc in next 8 sts], dc in each of next 3 tr fp; repeat from * 2 more times; repeat between [ ], join, fasten off.

Rnd 7: Working around ch-3 on last 2 rnds at the same time, join white with sl st in any corner ch-3 sp, (ch 3, 2 dc, ch 3, 3 dc) in same sp, dc in next 19 sts, *(3 dc, ch 3, 3 dc) in next ch sp, dc in next 19 sts; repeat from * around, join, fasten off.

To **join Blocks,** hold two Blocks right sides together, matching sts and ch sps; working through both thicknesses, join white with sc in top right corner ch sp, sc in same sp, sc in each st across to next corner ch sp, 2 sc in corner ch sp, fasten off.

Repeat with remaining Blocks, making five strips of six Blocks each.

To **join strips,** holding two strips right sides together, matching sts, seams and ch sps, join white with sc in first ch sp, sc in same sp, sc in each st and in each seam across with 2 sc in each ch sp, fasten off. Repeat with remaining strips.

Border
Rnd 1: Working around entire outer edge,

Continued on page 155

Antique Roses

joni sheedy, designer

An artful combination of roses and brown lend a romantic quality to this exquisite coverlet. Graceful and elegant, it's a valuable asset to any decor.

Finished Size
52" x 75"

Materials
Worsted-weight yarn — 15 oz. each lt. rose and dk. rose, 11 oz. brown; J crochet hook or size needed to obtain gauge.

Gauge
5 dc sts = 2"; 3 dc rows = 2".

Skill Level
★★ Average

Instructions
Block No. 1 (make 4)
Rnd 1: With lt. rose, ch 2, 8 sc in 2nd ch from hook, join with sl st in first sc (8 sc).

Rnd 2: Ch 3, dc in same st, 2 dc in each st around, join with sl st in top of ch-3, fasten off (16 dc).

Rnd 3: Join dk. rose with sl st in any st, ch 4, dc in same st, skip next st, *(dc, ch 1, dc) in next st, skip next st; repeat from * around, join with sl st in 3rd ch of ch-4.

Rnd 4: (Sl st, ch 3, 2 dc, ch 2, 3 dc) in next ch-1 sp, ch 1, 3 dc in next ch-1 sp, ch 1, *(3 dc, ch 2, 3 dc) in next ch-1 sp, ch 1, 3 dc in next ch-1 sp, ch 1; repeat from * around, join with sl st in top of ch-3, fasten off.

Rnd 5: Join brown with sl st in any corner ch-2 sp, (ch 3, 2 dc, ch 2, 3 dc) in same sp, ch 1, (3 dc, ch 1) in each ch-1 sp around with (3 dc, ch 2, 3 dc, ch 1) in each corner ch-2 sp, join.

Rnd 6: Sl st in each of next 2 sts, (sl st, ch 3, 2 dc, ch 2, 3 dc) in next corner ch sp, ch 1, (3 dc, ch 1) in each ch-1 sp around with (3 dc, ch 2, 3 dc, ch 1) in each corner ch-2 sp, join, fasten off.

Rnd 7: With lt. rose, repeat rnd 5.

Rnd 8: Repeat rnd 6, **do not** fasten off.

Rnd 9: Repeat rnd 6.

Rnd 10: With dk. rose, repeat rnd 5.

Rnd 11: Repeat rnd 6, **do not** fasten off.

Rnd 12: Repeat rnd 6.

Rnd 13: Repeat rnd 5.

Rnd 14: Ch 3, dc in each st and in each ch-1 around with 3 dc in each corner ch-2 sp, join, fasten off (200).

Rnd 15: For **flower,** working in **front lps** *(see fig. 1, pg. 158)* of skipped sts on rnd 2, join lt. rose with sc in any st, 9 sc in same st, 10 sc in each skipped st around, join with sl st in first sc, fasten off.

Block No. 2 (make 2)
Reversing lt. and dk. rose, work same as Block No. 1.

Assembly
Hold Blocks wrong sides together, matching sts; working in **back lps** through both thicknesses from one center corner st to next center corner st, alternating colors, with brown, sl st Blocks together in two rows of three Blocks each.

Working in **fronts lps** of rnd 15 on each block, join same color rose as flower center in any st, sl st in each st around, join with sl st in first sl st, fasten off.

Border
Rnd 1: Working around entire outer edge in **back lps** only, join brown with sl st in any st, ch 3, dc in each st and in each seam

Continued on page 155

Rosy Glow

jan hatfield, designer

Bring regal elegance to your home with this delicately ruffled throw. Its radiant sophistication will be a treasured gift for all to admire and enjoy.

Finished Size
52" x 66"

Materials
Worsted-weight yarn — 38 oz. white, 30 oz. pink; tapestry needle; H crochet hook or size needed to obtain gauge.

Gauge
Rnds 1-3 = 3½" across.
Each Block is 7" square.

Skill Level
★ Easy

Instructions
Block (make 63)

Rnd 1: With pink, ch 4, 11 dc in 4th ch from hook, join with sl st in top of ch-3 (12 dc).

Rnd 2: Ch 3, dc in same st, 2 dc in each st around, join, fasten off (24).

Note: For **treble front post (tr fp),** yo 2 times, insert hook from front to back around post *(see fig. 9, pg. 159)* of indicated st on rnd below; complete as tr.

Rnd 3: Join white with sl st in 2nd st, ch 3, dc in same st, tr fp around corresponding st on rnd before last, skip next st, (2 dc in next st, tr fp around corresponding st on rnd before last, skip next st) around, join (24 dc, 12 tr fp).

Rnd 4: Sl st in next dc, (sl st, ch 1, sc) in next tr fp, ch 3, skip next 2 dc, (sc in next tr fp, ch 3, skip next 2 dc) around, join with sl st in first sc, fasten off.

Rnd 5: Join pink with sl st in any ch-3 sp, ch 3, 2 dc in same sp, tr fp around next tr fp on rnd before last, (3 dc in next ch sp on this rnd, tr fp around next tr fp on rnd before last) around, join with sl st in top of ch-3, fasten off.

Rnd 6: Join white with sl st in any tr fp, (ch 3, 2 dc, ch 1, 3 dc) in same st, 3 dc in each of next 2 tr fp, *(3 dc, ch 1, 3 dc) in next tr fp, 3 dc in each of next 2 tr fp; repeat from * around, join, fasten off.

Rnd 7: Join pink with sl st in any corner ch-1 sp, (ch 3, 3 dc, ch 1, 4 dc) in same sp, *[tr fp around center dc of next 3-dc group on rnd before last, (3 dc in center st of next 3-dc group on this rnd, tr fp around center dc of next 3-dc group on rnd before last) 2 times], (4 dc, ch 1, 4 dc) in next ch-1 sp on this rnd; repeat from * 2 more times; repeat between [ ], join, fasten off.

Rnd 8: Join white with sl st in any ch-1 sp, (ch 3, 4 dc, ch 1, 5 dc) in same sp, *[tr fp around next tr fp on last rnd, (3 dc in center dc of next 3-dc group on this rnd, tr fp around next tr fp on last rnd) 2 times], (5 dc, ch 1, 5 dc) in next ch-1 sp on this rnd; repeat from * 2 more times; repeat between [ ], join, fasten off.

Hold Blocks wrong sides together, matching sts; working in **back lps** *(see fig. 1, pg. 158),* with white, sew together in seven rows of nine Blocks each.

Ruffle

Rnd 1: Working around entire outer edge in **back lps** only, join pink with sl st in any st, sl st in each st and in each ch around with ch-1 over each seam, join with sl st in first sl st, fasten off.

Continued on page 155

Sugar & Spice

Continued from page 146

Edging

Row 1: Working on one long edge of Strip, join ecru with sc in ch-3 sp at bottom right-hand corner, sc in each st, sc in each ch-3 sp on each side of seams and hdc in each seam across with sc in top right-hand corner ch-3 sp, turn (239 sts).

Row 2: Ch 1, sc in first st, (ch 1, skip next st, sc in next st) across, turn, fasten off.

Row 3: Join lt. gold with sl st in first st, ch 3, dc in each ch sp and in each st across, **do not** turn, fasten off.

Note: For **front post stitch (fp)** *(see fig. 1, pg. 158)*, yo, insert hook from front to back around post of st on previous row, complete as dc.

Row 4: Join ecru with sl st in first st, ch 3, (fp around next st, dc in next st) across, turn.

Row 5: Ch 1, sc in first st, (ch 1, skip next st, sc in next st) across, turn, fasten off.

Row 6: Join white with sc in first st, sc in next ch-1 sp, (ch 1, skip next st, sc in next ch-1 sp) across to last st, sc in last st, fasten off.

Strips No. 2-4
Block (make 10)

Work same as Strip No. 1 Block.

Edging

Work same as Strip No. 1 Edging.

Joining in ch-3 sp on top left-hand corner of Strip and working to bottom left-hand corner ch sp, repeat Edging on opposite long edge.

Strip No. 5
Block (make 10)

Work same as Strip No. 1 Block.

Edging

Joining in ch-3 sp on top left-hand corner of Strip and working to bottom left-hand corner ch sp, work same as Strip No. 1 Edging.

Assembly

Hold Strips wrong sides tog, matching sts on Edging; working in **back lps,** sew together.

Border

Rnd 1: Working around entire outer edge, join ecru with sc in ch-3 sp at top left-hand corner, ch 3, sc in same sp, sc in each st, sc in each seam, sc in each ch sp, sc in end of each sc row and 2 sc in end of each dc row around with (sc, ch 3, sc) in each corner ch sp, join with sl st in first sc, **turn** (183 sc on each short end, 241 sc on each long edge, 4 ch-3 sps).

Rnd 2: Sl st in next st, ch 1, sc in same st, *ch 1, skip next st, (sc in next st, ch 1, skip next st) across to next corner ch sp, (sc, ch 3, sc) in next ch sp; repeat from * 3 more times, ch 1, join, **turn,** fasten off.

Rnd 3: Join lt. gold with sl st in any corner ch-3 sp, (ch 3, dc, ch 2, 2 dc) in same sp, dc in each st and in each ch-1 sp around with (2 dc, ch 2, 2 dc) in each corner ch sp, join with sl st in top of ch-3, fasten off.

Rnd 4: Join ecru with sl st in any corner ch-2 sp, (ch 3, dc, ch 2, 2 dc) in same sp, *[dc in next st, (fp around next st, dc in next st) across to next corner], (2 dc, ch 2, 2 dc) in next corner ch sp; repeat from * 2 more times; repeat between [ ], join, **turn.**

Rnd 5: Sl st in next st, ch 1, sc in same st, *(ch 1, skip next st, sc in next st) across to next corner ch sp, (sc, ch 3, sc) in next ch sp, sc in next st; repeat from * 3 more times, ch 1, join with sl st in first sc, **turn,** fasten off.

Rnd 6: Join white with sc in any corner ch sp, ch 3, sc in same sp, *[sc in next st, (ch 1, skip next st, sc in next ch sp) across to next corner, ch 1, skip next st, sc in next st], (sc, ch 3, sc) in next corner ch sp; repeat from * 2 more times; repeat between [ ], join, **do not** turn.

Rnd 7: Ch 1, sc in each st and in each ch-1 sp around with (sc, ch 3, sc) in each corner ch-3 sp, join, **turn.**

Rnd 8: Ch 1, sc in first st, *ch 1, skip next st, (sc in next st, ch 1, skip next st) across to next corner ch-3 sp, (sc, ch 3, sc) in next ch sp; repeat from * 3 more times, ch 1, join, **turn.**

Rnd 9: (Sl st, ch 1, sc, ch 2, sc) in next ch-1 sp, (sc, ch 2, sc) in each ch-1 sp around with (sc, ch 2, sc, ch 3, sc, ch 2, sc) in each corner ch-3 sp, join, fasten off.✤

Native Sunset

Continued from page 149

join white with sl st in any st, ch 3, dc in each st, 2 dc in each ch sp on each side of seams and dc in each seam around with (3 dc, ch 3, 3 dc) in each corner ch-3 sp, join with sl st in top of ch-3, fasten off.

Rnd 2: Join turquoise with sl st in any dc, ch 3, dc in each st around with (3 dc, ch 3, 3 dc) in each corner ch-3 sp, join, fasten off.

Fringe

For **each Fringe,** cut eight strands each 12" long. With all strands held together, fold in half, insert hook in st, draw fold through, draw all loose ends through fold, tighten. Trim ends.

Alternating colors, evenly space 21 Fringe across each short end of afghan.✤

Antique Roses

Continued from page 151

around with 3 dc in each corner st, join with sl st in top of ch-3 (520 dc).

Note: For **cross stitch (cr st),** skip next st, dc in next st; working over dc just made, dc in skipped st.

Rnd 2: Working this rnd in **back lps,** ch 3, working over ch-3, dc in st before ch-3, cr st around, join.

Rnd 3: Working this rnd in **back lps,** ch 3, dc in each st around with 5 dc in each corner, join, fasten off (536).

Rnd 4: Join lt. rose with sl st in any st, ch 3, dc in each st around with 5 dc in each center corner st, join, fasten off (552).

Rnd 5: With dk. rose, repeat rnd 4, **do not** fasten off (568).

Rnd 6: Ch 3, dc in same st, dc in each st around with 5 dc in each center corner st, join, fasten off (585).

Rnd 7: Join lt. rose with sl st in sp between 2 sts at one corner, (ch 3, 2 dc, ch 2, 3 dc) in same sp, ch 1; working in space between sts, (skip next 3 sts, 3 dc in next sp, ch 1) around with (3 dc, ch 2, 3 dc, ch 1) in each corner sp, join, fasten off.

Rnd 8: Join dk. rose with sl st in any ch-1 sp, ch 3, 2 dc in same sp, 3 dc in each ch-1 sp around with (3 dc, ch 2, 3 dc) in each corner ch-2 sp, join.

Rnd 9: Working in sps between sts, ch 1, sc in each sp around with 3 sc in each corner ch-2 sp, join with sl st in first sc.

Rnd 10: Ch 1, **reverse sc** *(see fig. 10, pg. 159)* in each st around, join with sl st in first sc, fasten off.

Rnd 11: Working this rnd in **front lps** of rnd 1 on Border, join lt. rose with sl st in any st, sl st in each st around, join with sl st in first sl st, fasten off.

Rnd 12: Working in **front lps** of rnd 2, with dk. rose, repeat rnd 11.✤

Rosy Glow

Continued from page 152

Rnd 2: Working this rnd in **back lps,** join white with sl st in any st, ch 3, 2 dc in same st, 3 dc in each st around, join with sl st in top of ch-3.

Rnd 3: Ch 3, dc in each st around, join, fasten off.

Rnd 4: Join pink with sc in any st, ch 2, skip next st, (sc in next st, ch 2, skip next st) around, join with sl st in first sc, fasten off.✤

General Instructions

Yarn & Hooks

When shopping for yarn, be sure to check the label for the weight specification. By using the weight of yarn specified in the pattern, you will be assured of achieving the proper gauge. It is best to purchase at least one extra skein of each color needed to allow for differences in tension and dyes.

The hook size stated in the pattern is to be used as a guide for determining the hook size you will need. Always work a swatch of an afghan's stitch pattern with the suggested hook size. If you find your gauge is smaller or larger than what is specified in the pattern, choose a different size hook.

Gauge

Gauge is measured by counting the number of rows or stitches per inch. Each of the afghans featured in this book will have a gauge listed. In some patterns, gauge for small motifs or flowers is given as an overall measurement. Gauge must be attained in

order for the afghan to come out the size stated, and to prevent ruffling and puckering.

Make a swatch about 4" square in the stitch indicated in the gauge section of the instructions. Lay the swatch flat and measure the stitches. If you have more stitches per inch than specified in the pattern, your gauge is too tight and you need a larger hook. Fewer stitches per inch indicates a gauge that is too loose. In this case, choose the next smaller hook size.

Next, check the number of rows. Generally, if the stitch gauge is achieved, the row gauge will also be correct. However, due to differing crochet techniques and hook styles, you may need to adjust your gauge slightly by pulling the loops down a little tighter on your hook, or by pulling your loops up slightly to extend them.

Once you've attained the proper gauge, you're ready to start your afghan. Remember to check your gauge periodically to avoid problems when it's time to assemble the pieces, or to prevent the edges of your afghan from having a wavy appearance.

Pattern Repeat Symbols

Written crochet instructions typically include symbols such as parentheses, asterisks and brackets. In some patterns, a fourth symbol, usually a diamond, may be added. These symbols are used as signposts to set off a portion of instructions that will be worked more than once.

( ) Parentheses enclose instructions which are to be worked the number of times indicated after the parentheses. For example, "(2 dc in next st, skip next st) 5 times" means to follow the instructions within the parentheses a total of five times. Parentheses may also be used to enclose a group of stitches which should be worked in one space or stitch. For example, "(2 dc, ch 2, 2 dc) in next st" means to work all the stitches within the parentheses in the next stitch.

* Asterisks may be used alone or in pairs, many times in combination with parentheses. If used in pairs, a set of instructions enclosed within asterisks will be followed by instructions for repeating. These repeat instructions

may appear later in the pattern or immediately after the last asterisk. For example, "*Dc in next 4 sts, (2 dc, ch 2, 2 dc) in corner sp*, dc in next 4 sts; repeat between ** 2 more times" means to work through the instructions up to the word "repeat," then repeat only the instructions that are enclosed within the asterisks twice.

If used alone an asterisk marks the beginning of instructions which are to be repeated. For example, "Ch 2, dc in same st, ch 2, *dc in next st, (ch 2, skip next 2 sts, dc in next st) 5 times; repeat from * across" means to work from the beginning, then repeat only the instructions after the *, working all the way across the row. Instructions for repeating may also specify a number of times to repeat, followed by further instructions. In this instance, work through the instructions one time, then repeat the number of times stated, then follow the remainder of the instructions.

[ ] Brackets and ◊ diamonds are used in the same manner as asterisks. Follow the specific instructions given when repeating. Sometimes, all four repeat symbols will appear in the same row or round. There is no need to be intimidated by this. When followed carefully, these signposts will get you where your going — to the end of a beautiful finished project.

Finishing

Patterns that require assembly will suggest a tapestry needle in the materials. This should be a #16 or #18 blunt-tipped tapestry needle. Sharp-pointed needles are not appropriate, as they can cut the yarn and weaken the stitches. When stitching pieces together, be careful to keep the seams flat so pieces do not pucker at the seams.

Hiding loose ends is never a fun task, but if done correctly, may mean the difference between an afghan that looks great for years,

or one that soon shows signs of wear. Always leave about 6-8" when beginning or ending. Thread the loose end into your tapestry needle and carefully weave the end through the back of several stitches. Then, to assure a secure hold, weave in the opposite direction, going through different strands. Gently pull the end, and clip, allowing the end to pull up under the stitches.

If your afghan needs blocking, a light steam pressing works well. Lay your afghan on a large table or on the floor, shaping and smoothing by hand as much as possible. Adjust your steam iron to the permanent press setting, then hold slightly above the stitches, allowing the steam to penetrate the yarn. Do not rest the iron on the afghan. Allow to dry completely.

Most afghans do not require professional blocking, but if this is your preference, choose a cleaning service that specializes in needlework. Request blocking only if you do not want the afghan dry cleaned, and attach fringe or tassels after blocking.

Our sincerest thanks and appreciation goes to Coats & Clark and Spinrite for generously providing their product for use in the following projects:

Coats & Clark
Sunburst
Flowers on Parade
Perennial Medley
Peach Parfait
Evening Stars
Autumn Lights
Razzle Dazzle

Strawberry Sundae
Desert Flower
Ocean Waves
Shades of Green
Coral Blossoms
English Garden
Celestial Lights
Holiday Squares & Stripes

Floral Delight
Tropical Lagoon
Bluebells
Sugar & Spice

Spinrite
Cabbage Roses
Granny's Sweetheart

Stitch Guide

BASIC STITCHES

1 Front Loop (A)/Back Loop (B)
(front lp/back lp)

2 Chain
(ch)

Yo, draw hook through lp.

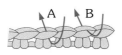

3 Slip Stitch
(sl st)

Insert hook in st, yo, draw through st and lp on hook.

4 Single Crochet
(sc)

Insert hook in st (A), yo, draw lp through, yo, draw through both lps on hook (B).

5 Half Double Crochet
(hdc)

Yo, insert hook in st (A), yo, draw lp through (B), yo, draw through all 3 lps on hook (C).

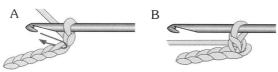

6 Double Crochet
(dc)

Yo, insert hook in st (A), yo, draw lp through (B), (yo, draw through 2 lps on hook) 2 times (C and D).

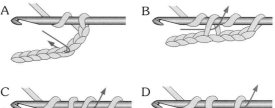

7 Treble Crochet
(tr)

Yo 2 times, insert hook in st (A), yo, draw lp through (B), (yo, draw through 2 lps on hook) 3 times (C, D and E).

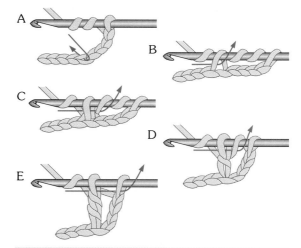

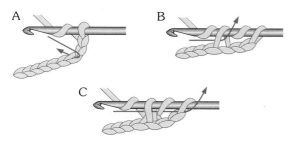

Standard Stitch Abbreviations

ch(s)	chain(s)
dc	double crochet
dtr	double treble crochet
hdc	half double crochet
lp(s)	loop(s)
rnd(s)	round(s)
sc	single crochet
sl st	slip stitch
sp(s)	space(s)
st(s)	stitch(es)
tog	together
tr	treble crochet
tr tr	triple treble crochet
yo	yarn over

8. Double Treble Crochet (dtr)

Yo 3 times, insert hook in st (A), yo, draw lp through (B), (yo, draw through 2 lps on hook) 4 times (C, D, E and F).

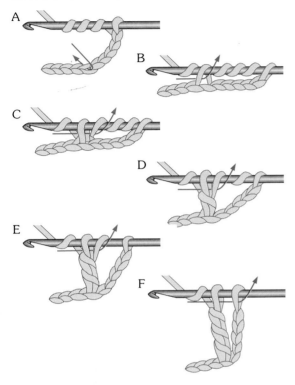

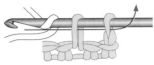

CHANGING COLORS

11. Single Crochet Color Change (sc color change)

Drop first color; yo with 2nd color, draw through last 2 lps of st.

12. Double Crochet Color Change (dc color change)

Drop first color; yo with 2nd color, draw through last 2 lps of st.

DECREASING

13. Single Crochet next 2 stitches together (sc next 2 sts tog)

Draw up lp in each of next 2 sts, yo, draw through all 3 lps on hook.

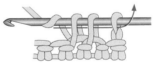

14. Half Double Crochet next 2 stitches together (hdc next 2 sts tog)

(Yo, insert hook in next st, yo, draw lp through) 2 times, yo, draw through all 5 lps on hook.

15. Double Crochet next 2 stitches together (dc next 2 sts tog)

(Yo, insert hook in next st, yo, draw lp through, yo, draw through 2 lps on hook) 2 times, yo, draw through all 3 lps on hook.

SPECIAL STITCHES

9. Front Post/Back Post Stitches (fp/bp)

Yo, insert hook from front to back (A) or back to front (B) around post of st on indicated row; complete as stated in pattern.

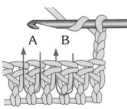

10. Reverse Single Crochet (reverse sc)

Working from left to right, insert hook in next st to the right (A), yo, draw through st, complete as sc (B).

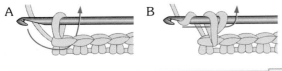

Index